To, Martin O'Brien

One Place...One Time

A memoir of Tuam in the 1930's & 40's

With best wishes from
Tommy Kelly

Thomas Kelly

Email: tbkelly@eircom.net

Published by:
Shruffaun Publishing, Newcastle, Galway.

ISBN: 978-0-9564449-2-9

Book Layout:
Stone Lakes Design
www.stonelakesdesign.ie

Printed by:
Snap Galway
www.snapgalway.ie

In Memory of Michael and Norah Kelly

Contents

1. Preface

In his book, *A Time for Voices,* Brendan Kennelly refers to experience as 'a matter of bits and pieces, flickers, glimpses, fragments, things half-remembered'. In the following pages I have attempted to gather together some personal bits and pieces from the years I spent in the town of Tuam during the 1930's and 1940's. I hope that in doing so I may convey some sense of what it was like to grow up in the town that I knew and shared with my generation, the generation that has been labelled the silent generation by some sociologists. It was an era in which the social and economic environments were dominated by the protectionist policies of church and state. Ireland was then a relatively new state operating in the shadows of the Civil War and the far-reaching Great Depression and engaging in an economic war with its nearest neighbour and main trading partner whilst the clouds of another war were gathering in mainland Europe. My primary school years coincided with that war so that Ireland's neutral stance more or less cut us off from the rest of the world. It was a period of many restrictions and scarcities which we accepted as normal and our adolescent years were a time of slow and stringent recovery from that prolonged period of austerity.

The experiences of those years in Tuam have continued to be important reference points for me even though I have lived in many places since then and have extended my horizons a little in the process. I envy those who keep a diary of their daily doings from which they can retrospectively glean a fuller picture of events. I didn't have that discipline so this personal account is compiled mainly by trawling a sea of fading memories but supported by reference to various articles written about Tuam from time to time including events reported in the local newspaper. It is also laced with a considerable amount of mature reflection, to coin a phrase.

As people get older recollecting experiences of the past is a common feature of their dialogue with friends and acquaintances. Some will be encouraged to record their version of events after such a nostalgic session. Others may have a personal urge to do so but find that it is easier said than done. Talk comes easy in convivial company especially if there is someone prepared to listen but putting pen to paper can be an inhibiting task which is often neglected until the stories are lost. It is my opinion that many people of my own and earlier generations were conditioned into believing that the business of writing was best left to the experts and the scholars and that what is worth recording relates only to the lives of celebrities and the activities with which they are associated. But we can learn much from the lives and experiences of ordinary people who also have real stories to tell.

The achievements of the leading lights in the town's past have been well documented elsewhere by those competent to do so. My particular interest is in recalling how the ordinary inhabitants of the town, my own people got on with living their lives. Those lives have not been written about to any great extent and most of what I know of them has been obtained through personal contact and handed down through the oral medium. I have gone to school and have met some scholars in my time but much of my own basic knowledge of the world derives from my early encounters with ordinary people who haven't made any claims to distinction or featured in the headlines, whose wisdom was acquired without the benefits of the formal educational opportunities available to the present-day generations but whose influence continues to ripple through the society which they helped to build.

I believe that I was lucky enough to be part of a community which succeeded, to a considerable extent, in protecting its young from the hardships endured by previous generations and in sheltering them from the more traumatic stresses and strains of daily life. Whilst our elders, in their mainly god-fearing and law-abiding ways, got on with the business of working to make ends meet it was, by and large, left to the politicians, the churchmen, the people of property and the professionals to run things from their positions of power and influence. Social networking for working class people did not extend much beyond one's immediate neighbourhood and mentoring in the ways of the world consisted to a large extent in what was picked up in the home and its environs.

The educational policies in operation at the time facilitated the early exodus of many young people, with potential, from the school system. Until the Vocational Education Act of 1930 came into being the state had not become involved in the provision of second level schools and it was left to the churches and religious orders to do so. Those who made it to second level were therefore considered to be privileged and those of us who were able to avail of such privilege are indebted to the members of those orders who, through their work, subsidised and propped up the secondary schools until the state eventually faced up to its responsibilities in that respect. Only those who gained scholarships or who could afford it made it to third level. Many of my contemporaries went into the world of work at the age of fourteen believing that school had little more to offer them in preparation for the real world. Those who were fortunate enough to get apprenticeships in trades and business continued their education in those areas and many made good lives for themselves at home and away. Others took whatever casual work was available for the time being to supplement family incomes until something more permanent came along or until they were old enough to follow their older brothers and sisters on the emigrant trail. The prospect of emigration was almost taken for granted and there seemed to be an acceptance that the future for many would be acted out elsewhere. I remember a teacher in school telling us that Irish people were the possessors of *féith na fániochta*, the vein of wanderlust. This was a colourful, almost romantic sound bite, useful as a quotation in essays on the topic of emigration, but a facile summary of its reality.

With the benefit of hindsight, and at a remove in time and distance, I have come to a better understanding of that world and of its social undercurrents. Silver spoons were very scarce even when there was a weekly wage coming into a house. When illness or unemployment or both showed their ugly heads life was hard for old and young in an era when social welfare was very limited in scope. As in every generation there were those in comfortable positions with sufficient power to influence how others were expected to live their lives. But those in the upper echelons did not have a monopoly of wisdom, ability or integrity. I realise, sadly, how harshly some young people, especially those from the less well-off sections of society, were dealt with by the authorities of the time for what would today be considered minor misdemeanours. All I can say is that they would have been dealt with much more kindly if it had been left to their peers to judge them. When petty snobbery was encountered I like to think that it was treated with an appropriate amount of justifiable disdain.

I have only hazy recollections of the thirties in Tuam but certain events flicker through that haze from time to time. One of my earliest memories is of the day my father cut my hair for the first time against the wishes of my older sisters who enjoyed tending the long tresses which I sported at that time. This ritual took place while seated on an upturned orange-box on the kitchen table. It was the first rite of passage into the male world and an ordeal which I hated until eventually I graduated to Robert Holmes' barber shop on the Ballygaddy Road where haircuts for boys were four pence and where you listened to the issues of the day being discussed as you awaited your turn in the queue. I also remember on my fourth birthday getting a small paper-bag of ginger snaps in Mrs Forde's shop which was next door to us in St Paul's Terrace. I had a 'feast' sitting on the kerb-stone of the footpath outside our house assisted by Billy Murphy who lived across the street.

As we spread our wings the street, with its adjoining fields and vacant sites, became an important part of our childhood world. A street such as Church View was an important element in the lives of town children as it was there we played and laughed and learned to interact with other children even before we started school, and there was no shortage of children of all ages to play with. We were unaware that technically we were not entitled to play on the public thoroughfare or in the open spaces but that was long before the concept of civic recreational amenities was on the agenda. What we never knew didn't bother us and we got on with life and had fun. Just recently I read of a sociological study which found that children who played in the open laughed much more than those who played indoors even with the benefit of all sorts of modern toys and technology. And it is accepted that laughter is good medicine. I suppose we were lucky in the sense that the streets at that time were safe areas and we were never far from home or the watchful gaze of our stay-at-home mothers or older siblings.

Amongst the children street games were popular and knowledge of them was passed on from older to younger children. This was an important part of the socialisation process for the small children who were initiated into the various activities by the older children. Those games were mainly played by the girls and the smaller boys who were docile enough to be hauled into them to make

My sisters: Noreen, Eileen, Bridie and Margaret

up the numbers. Rhymes were a feature of the games and were used to determine the order of play or in the selection of participants. Many of those rhymes were handed down from generation to generation and were not particular to Tuam. The earliest memory I have of such games is holding hands with other children and going round in a circle singing

'Ring-a-ring a Rosie, a pocket full of Posies,

Atishoo, atishoo, we all fall down.'

All that was needed for such games as 'Redlight' and 'Giant Steps' was a convenient gable-end. All available to play would be lined up against Leahy's gable and various rhymes, like the following, would be recited to eliminate players one by one:

'Eeny, meeny, miney mo, catch a body by the toe,

If he screeches let him go, eeny meeny miney mo'.

Another such rhyme was

'Ikil, akil black bottle, ikil, akil out

O, U, T, spells OUT and out of this game you must go.'

The more assertive children would command first call saying 'I'm first ikil' and 'I'm second ikil' and often there would be rows in the rush to see who would get the first call. We had all the rhymes off by heart and they were as familiar to us as our prayers. We even had a rhyme to deal with the weather when it interfered with our play:

'Rain, rain, go away, come another washing day!'

It may never have worked but it was always worth a try. If any children came to the street on holidays to stay with relatives they would be enlisted into the play and usually added their own variations to the games. I remember a young boy and girl, a brother and sister, who came on holidays from England during the war years to stay with Mrs Forde who lived next door to us. They taught us a rhyme which fitted in perfectly with our own repertoire of street rhymes and which I can still recall. It went as follows:

'Eeena, meena, fakka, rakka, air, aye, donna, makka,

Seeka, muza, akka, akka, air, aye, bush.'

I remember the first day I went to school. My sister, Gabrielle and her pal May Kilkelly each held a hand until I was deposited safely in the babies' class in the Mercy Convent on the Dublin Road. Newcomers got a spin on a rocking horse which was produced on such occasions. It was hauled around the classroom by a big boy from 1st class. Mother Dominick gave us *marla* (plasticene) to play with and distributed slates on which we wrote letters and numbers with sticks of chalk. This was my first formal introduction to the three ' Rs'.

As I got to know the ropes I would walk home with older children until gradually I was able to negotiate the journey on my own down the Circular Road, past the Post Office then down Vicar Street and across the railway line at the station gates into home territory. Occasionally on the way home from school before turning into Circular Road I would break my journey. My aunt Nellie, who was also my godmother, worked as a housekeeper for Dr Thompson and his wife Eleanor Maude (nee Rutledge) in Eastland House on Dublin Road. I would climb what then seemed to be very high steps and was just about able to reach the polished brass knocker on the front door to announce my arrival. The house, at the time, had all the trappings of old decency with family portraits and ancient trophies decorating the walls. It was a typical upstairs, downstairs situation. Mrs Thompson, who was then widowed, would be sitting in her drawing room, off the hall with its highly polished linoleum, and my aunt would take me down stairs to her basement kitchen and give me tea or maybe lemonade and a biscuit. Mrs Thompson was quite elderly and hard of hearing by then but would be aware that there was a visitor below stairs. She would come to the top of the stairs and call out loudly to my aunt to bring the child up to her. She didn't have any children of her own nor did my aunt who was a single woman. She would talk to me and ask me questions about school and such before I would be eventually ushered out by my aunt and sent home. Maybe I flatter myself but, on reflection, I think that the occasional visit of a child might have brought a welcome diversion to the occupants of that particular house.

Mrs Thompson was a member of the Church of Ireland and when she died some years later I remember going to her funeral in what we always referred to as the Protestant Church in High St. She had no immediate relatives then living in Ireland and my aunt, as her faithful servant and companion over many years, was her chief mourner. What I remember clearly about that occasion was standing outside the church during the service which, as far as I know, was attended only by members of the Church of Ireland congregation whilst my tearful aunt and many of Mrs Thompson's Catholic friends and neighbours remained outside. Catholics were 'forbidden' to attend a Protestant service in those days and it was what was termed a 'reserved sin' to do so. One would be expected to go to a bishop or his nominee to be 'forgiven' if one dared to transgress. Thankfully, that scenario is long a thing of the past. In my opinion such episcopal bureaucracy intimidated good people who were totally loyal to their own church and belittled their personal entitlement to pay their final respects to an elderly, benevolent member of the broader community. Neither did it show any appreciation of the neighbourly relationships which existed between the vast majority of the townspeople of both traditions in their working and social lives.

Mrs Thompson and friend

I recall the nuns who taught me in those early years with varying degrees of affection, particularly Mother Dominick an elderly, motherly nun who taught us in the 'babies' class, Sr Cyril, then a young, friendly Kerry woman in 'high infants' and Sr Francis, a quiet-spoken, kindly nun in first class. I seem to have got on well with them and even after moving on to the Brothers and meeting them in later life remained friendly with them. There were boys and girls in 'babies' and 'high infants'. Some of the girls were resident in the Children's Home. They always walked as a group up the Dublin Road escorted by two women who lived in the Home. They disappeared from our lives after we graduated to first class where the boys were separated from the girls. I never knew them personally and can't recall ever hearing their names at roll call. It was only in later years that I became fully aware of the story of the Children's Home and of the social forces which determined how some people were forced to live their lives in that era. In our innocence we were oblivious of our ignorance. On the day we made our first communion we were treated to breakfast in the school after mass. We got mugs of tea and slices of loaf bread with rhubarb jam. We then got our class photograph taken in the convent grounds.

Mercy Convent First Communion Class 1940

Front Row: Mickey Eagleton, Gus Murray, Josie McHugh, Tommy Kelly, Patrick McGough, Billy Leahy, P.J. Ellicott, Paddy Mullins. 2nd Row: Sean Lohan, Joe Lohan, Eric Dooley, Mattie Mannion, Ted Lydon, Willie Douglas, Gerry Coady, P.M.Stapleton, Mick Barratt. Back Row: Tom Halligan, Sean Hogan, Christy Larkin, John Flynn, T.J. Kelly, Miko Ralph, Murt Burke, Bill Forde, Stephen Joyce,

3. Moving Out

Beyond the home and the street lay new experiences. I liked being taken for walks on Sunday afternoons by my father. My favourite journey was up through the town because there would be a stop for ice-cream at Molly Shine's shop opposite the Shruffaun near the station. No ice cream ever tasted as sweet and those childhood, summer Sundays seem to have been always fine. We often walked up along the railway line from the station gates, past the cemetery as far as the first bridge at the end of the houses on the Athenry Road and sometimes as far as Cloonascragh. On other occasions we went in the opposite direction, back the Claureen, down the railway line from Coughlan's gates and over the New Cut as far as the Beet Factory siding. For my father, who worked on the railway, it must have been something of a busman's holiday.

One Sunday we decided to take a short cut across a field to get out onto Ballygaddy Road. As we did so we were approached by a man who told us that we were trespassing on private property. My father was an inoffensive, mannerly man and responded in character. We quietly departed the holy ground and on our way home I asked him what was 'trespassing'. It was the first time that I had heard that word and he explained to me what it meant. Later at home I overheard him telling my mother about the encounter. I gathered from their conversation that he had been in the same class in school as the cross man who had accosted us. I still remember that encounter clearly. As well as learning the meaning of a new word I suspect it was my first inkling of the importance of '*The Field*' in the Irish psyche. I also got my first hint that the word 'class' has a variety of meanings several of which coincided on that occasion. My father and his erstwhile class-mate now occupy roughly the same amount of ground in the graveyard a short distance from that field. *Requiescant in pace.*

We often walked back the Weir Road, past the Killaloonty boreen, known locally as the *Léana* boreen, and on past a field called the 'Lawn' as far as the bridge over the Clare River (or the 'Wire' River as we called it). Close to the Lawn there was a field called the *Lisín* where miscarried babies and unbaptised infants had been buried. Some people claimed that the Lawn was haunted but I have no personal evidence of that claim. I always felt a sense of mystery in its vicinity. The road was not tarred at that time and on fine summer Sundays if a car passed it would leave a cloud of dust from the sanded road surface in its wake.

The Weirs bridge was a popular bathing place in summer. One Sunday there was a lot of commotion in the area. It turned out that a young man from the neighbourhood who had been swimming in the river had drowned. Even though I was just about five years old at the time I can still recall the feeling of gloom that enveloped the locality as a result of that tragic event. I remember his funeral procession passing up Church View some days afterwards. Some years ago when looking up the *Tuam Herald* for another purpose I came across an account of that incident which happened on the last Sunday of July (Reek Sunday) in 1938. The following extracts confirmed that I had not imagined the whole thing:

> 'Thomas Monaghan (20), Galway Road, Tuam, was drowned in the Weir River on Sunday last at about 4.30 p.m. This in brief is the story of the most shocking fatality in the town in recent years.

It appears that the youth was listening to the hurling match broadcast before going to the river with a friend, Miko Cannon. The latter, a good swimmer, crossed the river to the town side and, while he was there, Monaghan entered the water. He was only learning to swim and after a few minutes cried for help. His companion crossed the river, but by that time the deceased youth had been carried to the bridge where he sank.

Cannon, in a plucky rescue effort, caught the youth's swimming costume but was unable to hold him in the strong current.

Hearing the shouts, some men who were fishing in the vicinity, rushed to the bridge but were too late to render any assistance.

The Guards were summoned and three local youths, Jack Quinn, Vincent Stockwell and Eddie Ridge dived and swam around for over an hour in a vain attempt to locate the body.

On Monday, boats were procured and Guards and young men from the town worked in relays from early morning to late at night dragging the river. Owing to the recent heavy rain, the water had risen three or four feet, and this, with the strong current, has made the task of dragging very difficult. There is a large area of the surrounding land under water and the river is twice the normal width. Dragging was continued all day Tuesday and at 5.30 in the evening, success rewarded the efforts of the searchers. The body was located in about eight feet of water some 200 yards from the bridge and was brought up by Jack Quinn and Paddy Kelly.

When news spread that the body was recovered, crowds of people went to the Weir Bridge for the funeral. The coffin was carried by the young men of the town from the bridge to the Cathedral and the funeral cortege, which was the largest seen for years, stretched from the Galway Road corner to the Weir bridge.'

There are further details of the church ceremonies and of the inquest where Miko Cannon was commended for his efforts to save his friend. In a separate paragraph the paper commented on the need for a swimming pool in the town and on the fact that there was no boat available to help in the search. One had to be brought from Galway for that purpose. It is hard to believe that facilities for dealing with such an event were so lacking in what was a relatively large town. Even at this remove in time, I am struck by the poignancy of the situation and can only admire the young men, who, with nothing but their own strength of body and character, helped in the search. I knew them all when I was growing up without realising the significance of their deed and can only offer a belated salute to their memory. Ever after when we went to bathe at the Weirs bridge I had a fear of the river.

In later years I remember swimming galas being held there the highlight of which, for us kids, was when Paddy Kelly used to take part in the greasy pole competition and watching Jack Quinn from the Rustic Vaults diving from a high diving board erected for the occasion. These were two of the young men who had participated in the search for Tom Monaghan. As far as I remember those galas were organised by a man called John Henry Corcoran who owned a public house at the corner of Shop Street and Foster Place. He was also involved in a campaign to build a swimming pool in Tuam in the early forties. The swimming galas were later transferred to Ballygaddy which was a very popular bathing place. Diving from the bridge was a common activity on the part of the more daring chaps. For an inland town Tuam had many good swimmers but the facilities available then were fairly primitive. Bobby Burke was also very involved in trying to get a swimming pool for the town. Bobby was a good swimmer himself and used to take part in the diving competitions which were held in conjunction with the galas.

This photograph was taken outside Tighes's house at St Bridget's Terrace, The Claureen, during the construction of that terrace in the late 1920's.

Included are (back row) Jim Moggan, contractor, Jimmy O'Rourke, AN Other, John Byrne; (front row) John Greaney, AN Other, Malachy Lohan.

4. Intermission

During the summer of 1939 I went on my first holidays to a place my mother always called home. She came from the village of Ardhill in the parish of Roundfort in South Mayo and it was a great novelty for me, a child of the town, to spend summer holidays there with my Uncle Peter and my country cousins. I travelled on the train from Tuam to Hollymount with my Aunt Nora and on arrival was deposited in a friend's house close to the station whilst she walked the rest of the journey to her home three miles further on. Later that evening I was collected by my uncle in a horse and trap and transported on the last leg of the journey to my holiday destination. It was quite a culture shock to go from a crowded street to a place of open fields with the nearest house several fields away. It took time to adjust but children are adaptable if they have a sense of security. It was a novelty to be close to farm animals and to follow my cousins around as they carried out their farming chores. At night time I was ensconced on the hob by the open fire in the kitchen around which everyone, including visiting neighbours, sat and talked in the soft light of a paraffin oil lamp and the glow from the turf fire.

One Sunday, in early September, a cousin of mine came into the house and announced that 'the war is on'. I was vaguely aware of serious happenings in England because my eldest sister had recently gone there to become a trainee nurse and I was old enough to detect the concerns of my parents on her account but I didn't realise the significance of the major events taking place there and in Europe. The war was in full swing the following May when my schooling and childhood street games were interrupted and I departed Church View on my first train journey to Dublin.

For as long as I could remember I had been the object of particular attention from my parents and other adults. To be singled out, for any reason, in a family of ten gives a child a vague feeling of importance. Neighbours, uncles and aunts, the local midwife, the bonesetter and even the doctor were, at various times, brought into the deliberations. I was usually made to march up and down the room whilst the current consultant gave his or her opinion. There never seemed to be unanimity on the matter. The females always seemed to agree with my mother that something should be done. The males, taking their cue from my father, usually said 'there's nothing wrong with the child and you should leave well enough alone'. Eventually the classical compromise was reached, my mother's opinion prevailed and arrangements were made for me to go to the Richmond Hospital in Dublin.

The journey to Dublin is just a blurred memory but I remember, as the train trundled across the bridge over the river Shannon at Athlone, my father telling me that this was the biggest river in Ireland and that we were now leaving the Province of Connacht. I clung to the strap on the carriage window fearful that the bridge might give way under us. When we arrived at Westland Row my maternal uncle, who was a member of the Garda Siochána in Dublin, met us and on the following day I was taken to the Richmond Hospital for what turned out to be a long drawn out and complicated orthopaedic experience. After several encounters with adults in white coats and blue uniforms I was taken by a nurse to a large room with a lot of beds in it where my parents were waiting to tell me that I would be staying there for a while. They explained to me that they would have to go home to mind the others but Uncle Tom would be in to see me often and it wouldn't be long until they would be coming to bring me home again and we would have another great spin on the train. I can't remember being too worried as they said goodbye. I didn't know then that it would be nine months before I would see them again.

The next morning a man with a trolley came and told me that he was taking me for a spin. After an exciting trip along corridors, through doors, around corners and along more corridors I was deposited in a room where there were several people with masks on. One of them came over and told me that she had a nice mask for me too. Placing it over my face she told me to take a deep breath. I felt that I was about to smother as I breathed in the ether which was then the normal method of putting one to sleep. The next thing I remember was waking up in the room where I had been that morning. I was sick from the effects of the ether and my left leg was tied to a contraption hanging from the ceiling over the bed and was encased in a white, rock-hard substance from waist to ankle. I remained in that position for several weeks.

As the days and weeks passed I had ample time to adjust to my new surroundings. I soon became attuned to the hospital sounds - the morning bedlam, crying children, rattling trolleys, footsteps and voices in the corridor outside the ward, bells announcing the end of visiting time. The footsteps and voices were a link with the outside world and in time I could determine which were likely to enter our world and which were going to pass by. I also began to recognise the sounds of the bustling city outside - church bells, the clip-clop of horses' hooves on cobbled streets and young voices at play in the schoolyard across the street which I later discovered was Brunswick Street C.B.S. where Paddy Crosby of *School around the Corner* fame later taught. Eventually they untied my leg and I was able to stretch out flat on the bed. However they didn't remove the white casing which was called plaster of Paris. Every time my uncle came in I asked when they would be taking the plaster off and each time he replied 'soon now'.

Gradually I gained a more extensive view of the world around me. Through the window opposite I could see high, smoking chimneys, church spires and a large green-domed building and I could see the outline of mountains in the distance. It was a welcome change from staring all day long at the ceiling in the hospital ward. I looked forward to any interruption in the monotony of the day's schedule. Apart from my uncle, visitors were few and far between. It was wartime Ireland and there were severe travel restrictions in place which meant that people only travelled if there was an emergency of some sort. Occasionally two girls, a bit older than myself, came and chatted with me. They never said who they were and I never asked them but I liked them because they always brought a little gift. I discovered, afterwards, that they were the children of a man who had worked on the railway with my father at one time and who had heard of me through that grapevine.

As time went by I became keenly aware of everything that went on around me. At one stage I noticed that an increasing number of the occupants were being taken from the ward. Overhearing conversations I gathered that an outbreak of diphtheria had occurred in Dublin and people suspected of contracting the disease were being transferred to a nearby fever hospital. One of the symptoms associated with the disease was nose-bleeding and when a patient displayed such symptoms they were tested and dispatched immediately to the nearby fever hospital. Several of the other patients had been transferred for this reason and I was rather disappointed that I wasn't one of the chosen ones as I longed for some variety in life. Realising that a nose-bleed was the key to a new life, I proceeded to do something about it and started working on my nose until eventually I drew blood. I called a nurse and pointed out that my nose was bleeding. She informed a doctor who carried out the routine tests and announced that I was to be transferred to the fever hospital. I was delighted as it entailed a short trip in an ambulance which was really exciting. When I arrived at the fever hospital I was deposited in the women's ward for whatever reason I never found out.

It was a new world of grown-ups of which I became an interested observer. The nurses and the female patients seemed to enjoy talking to one another in a language that I didn't quite understand. I remember an occasion when some of the nurses who were going to a dress dance came in to show off their style to the female patients. They paraded up and down the ward in their beautiful long gowns and high heeled shoes the likes of which I had never seen before. The aroma of perfume filled the ward and lingered long after their departure to the applause of the admiring female patients.

There was not a lot to excite a child there. I got plenty of attention from the female patients and even the nurses seemed to have more time for me than in the children's ward. I enjoyed the novelty of the change except for the fact that during that time I wasn't allowed any visitors at all. Whenever my Uncle Tom called, the nurses would carry me to the window of the ward from where I would wave to him below in the back lawn of the hospital grounds. On one such occasion he was accompanied by Nurse Connolly, the midwife from Tuam, who had delivered me and many of my contemporaries. She was visiting Dublin at the time and had called to see me but wasn't allowed in either.

The most exciting thing to happen while I was there was when a young woman left the hospital ward without permission. She was in a bed near me and during a quiet interlude she dressed and packed her belongings. I must have been the only one awake to what was happening and as she left she said she was going home and warned me not to say anything to anybody. Later that evening she was missed and there was a big hullabaloo. Everybody was quizzed but nobody had seen her leave.

One of the nurses asked me if I had seen her and I said that she was gone home. 'How do you know' asked the nurse. 'Because she told me', I replied. 'And why didn't you call us', she asked. 'Because she told me not to' I replied. I don't know how that story ended because after some weeks without any evidence of the disease manifesting itself I was transferred back to my old ward and to the old routine.

On occasions a friendly woman brought in books and on one of her visits she gave me a copy of *Just William* by Richmal Crompton which I really enjoyed. Each time she came after that she would have one of the 'William' books for me. Around Christmas time the two girl visitors brought me a game of *Snakes and Ladders* which their mother got for me when they were visiting Santa Claus in a place called Todd Burns. They showed me how to play and would play a few games with me before leaving. Around that time I also had a visit from a young woman from Tuam who brought me a present which my mother had sent. Her name was Maureen O'Brien who at the time was a nurse in Dublin and had been on a visit home to Tuam. Her father, Ned, was a railway man and a friend of my own father. I saw Maureen acting on the stage in the Town Hall many times in later years. On Christmas Day there was a concert and musical entertainment in the ward and some of the nurses and patients from other wards came in. One of the visitors sat beside my bed and spoke to me. It turned out that she was also from Tuam and she knew my father.

One evening shortly after Christmas there was a great commotion in the ward. Two nurses came in and drew the curtains over the windows. The lights were turned off and I could hear loud noises outside. There was a lot of hustle and bustle and sometime later some trolleys were wheeled in. Doctors and nurses, hidden behind screens with dull lights, were giving great attention to the newcomers. I could hear muffled talk from the adults and heard the word 'bombs' mentioned. Without realising it, I was having my first brush with the war. It was January 2nd 1941 and on that day a German plane had strayed from its bombing mission over Britain and had dropped bombs on Dublin. Two of them made direct hits on a place near the South Circular Road and over 20 people were injured. The new arrivals in the ward were some of the casualties. This incident helped to provide me with a degree of celebrity among the local children when I eventually returned home. I claimed that I had been in the war.

That homecoming was flagged one morning a couple of months later when a nurse arrived at my bedside with an instrument which resembled one that I had seen my Uncle Peter using for shearing sheep. She proceeded to cut away at the plaster casing on my leg starting at the ankle all the way up the length of my leg to my hip. With her final cut the plaster split open and the leg was revealed. It was red and raw and very tender to the touch. She replaced the plaster with a bandage and then helped me to put my feet on the ground for the first time in nine months.

It took me some time to adapt to this new-found freedom to walk about. A few days later my Uncle Tom came in and said we were going home. He helped me to pack my belongings which consisted mainly of a cardboard box containing a game of *Snakes and Ladders*. He then took me out to a large black car and put me in the back seat whilst he sat in the front with the driver. This was a special treat, as cars were a very scarce commodity in Dublin at the time. I was not aware of that fact, or that I was being chauffeured from the Richmond Hospital to Westland Row at the expense of the state. Uncle Tom had arranged the lift from one of his mates in the Garda Depot in the Phoenix Park and I was now sitting in the seat normally occupied by the then Minister for Defence, one Oscar Traynor, T D. As we drove in state through the streets of Dublin I felt a little sad to be leaving behind the things that

I had become accustomed to but I was looking forward to the train journey home.

It's a small world. On the journey home a gentleman who boarded the train at Mullingar got into conversation with my uncle. It turned out that he was originally from Tuam and had been in school with my father. He was a Mr. Dempsey from Athenry and when he was leaving he gave me a two-shilling piece. When we reached Tuam we walked from the station to our house in Church View. Several of the children from the street were waiting at the Tierboy Road corner and escorted me on the last lap of the journey home where my mother and several of the local women were waiting to greet me. My father and the men of the street were probably at work. I think we had a bit of a party and for a while I was an object of curiosity at home and among the neighbours' children.

I was soon back down to earth when I returned to spend my last few months in the Mercy convent after my sojourn in hospital. Shortly afterwards it was time to move to the Christian Brothers' school farther up the Dublin Road where, between primary and secondary school, I was to spend the next decade or so. There I met up with other graduates of the Mercy and boys who came from the Presentation convent. Many of my earlier classmates had moved a class ahead of me because of my extended stay in hospital but I caught up with a few of them later on. Whilst I felt a sense of having missed out on something as a result of that hiatus in my educational journey, it may have been an early, extended, sub-conscious lesson in getting to know oneself and in the virtue of patience when faced with situations beyond one's control.

Almost seventy years later, when I eventually got around to having the troublesome hip replaced with a brand new one, I asked the surgeon who carried out the operation if, in his opinion, the 9 months which I had spent, in plaster, as a child in the Richmond Hospital would have had any beneficial effect on the offending limb. After a brief pause he said quietly, and somewhat reluctantly, 'probably not'. Which only confirmed a long-held opinion of my own. Whether, or not, the experience had any ongoing psychological ramifications is a moot point.

First Class Mercy Convent c1940

Front Row: Tommy Kelly, Paschal Howard, Christy Fahy, Jack Hogan, Willie Douglas, Sylvester McTigue, Sean Holden, Denis Brennan. 2nd Row: Ted Lydon, Mattie Mannion, Miko Ralph, Jimmy Murray, John Flynn, Christy Larkin, Mickey Eagleton, James Corless, Sean Lohan, Paddy Mullins, John Ferguson. Back Row: Tom Halligan, Paschal Hogan, Bill Forde, Gerry Coady, Murt Burke, Jack McDonnell, Gus Cunningham, Joe Lohan, Mikey St John, Noel Monaghan.

My sister Bridie and myself on her First Holy Communion day.

5. On the Street where we lived

The Church View to which I returned after my sojourn in Dublin was a busy two-way thoroughfare extending from the Galway Road corner to the railway station. One of the first things that I noticed was the way people talked. In particular the way they said certain words like 'verra good' or 'verra bad'. It was the first time I became aware of the Tuam accent. On the other hand some of the children on the street said that I had a Dublin accent when I spoke. I'm sure that I must have picked up some of it over the nine months that I was exposed to it but it didn't take too long for me to revert to the local vernacular and to be re-immersed in the life of the street.

There was a large population of children of all ages and temperaments on our street and each was able to find his or her match quite easily in the mix. Rivalries sometimes caused friction and name calling and even occasional fist fights among the boys were not unknown. Cats and dogs were also plentiful and the dogs were always given full titles such as Rover Ryan or Spot Murphy or Blackface Mullins. Some people kept birds as pets and several houses had bird cages hanging outside their doors from which the sounds of canaries or goldfinches or yellow hammers mingled with the motley street sounds.

Many activities were associated with the different seasons of the year. With the approach of spring and the longer evenings, marbles, spinning tops, bowling hoops and skipping ropes made their appearance after their winter's hibernation. Marbles were prized possessions and acted as a form of currency in the barter systems that operated among the children as real pennies were scarce commodities. Glass marbles were more valuable than clay marbles but what the latter lacked in quality was made up for in quantity. Broken bits of delph and crockery called 'chainies' served a similar purpose among the girls who used them as 'legal tender' when playing 'shop'. Skipping ropes were very popular with the girls but were often commandeered by the

Miko Kelly, Tommy Murphy with friend

boys for playing cowboys. The 'cowboy' used the rope as the reins on the 'horse' as they galloped along the street in pairs. Hoops were also popular and often took the place of an imaginary horse as we bowled them along at full speed. Generally all that the hoop consisted of was an old bicycle wheel rim but on occasions we would get a wheel which still had the spokes intact. This was a much more valuable possession and if we could get one with a worn tyre on it we had a real 'Rolls Royce'.

In summer time the car-free street was ideal for those games and for less boisterous ones such as 'beds' (or hop-scotch as it was known in more sophisticated circles). This involved hopping on one leg through numbered boxes which were drawn with chalk on a suitable stretch of the road or on the footpath when it was eventually concreted. When real chalk was not available we used chunks of lime from old walls or gables which had been layered with whitewash over the years.

My first attempts at learning to cycle were on a bicycle owned by George Lyons. He was the only child on the street at that time who owned a small bike. It was a much envied possession of his and some of us would borrow it from time to time for practice. At that time young men and youths from out the country would park their bikes in 'safe houses' in Church View when coming to town on Sunday evenings to the pictures in the Mall cinema. To further our cycling prowess we would 'borrow' their bikes while they were enjoying the offerings of the silver screen. It was quite a feat to operate a man's bicycle from under the crossbar with the bicycle at a precarious angle from the perpendicular. In due course I was able to use my mother's bicycle without being able to reach the saddle of that machine until it was lowered to cater for my shortcomings.

During school holidays we would venture further afield to catch 'jaroges' and 'colyoges' in the New Cut. Jam jars were in great demand to house the catch and pre-dated the goldfish bowl. We also had summer time hikes to Cloonascragh when ringleaders like Baby O'Brien and Florrie McKenna would shepherd a batch of neighbourhood children to a picnic on the sandhills, the residue of eskers which were deposited there after the ice-age and from which the place derived its name. (*Eascracha* in Irish). There would also be an occasional trip during the summer on the Sunday excursion train to Galway with the added bonus of a dip in the salt water in Salthill. And no summer was complete in Church View without a stint in O'Connor's hayshed tramping the hay as it was brought in from the fields back the Weir Road. As the pile gradually grew higher in the large hayshed we were eventually able to swing from the rafters and tumble headlong into the freshly saved hay.

As the summer waned we turned our attention to picking mushrooms and blackberries in the fields around the town. There was a great feeling of satisfaction arriving home with a *tráithnín* chain of freshly picked mushrooms.

A particular attraction on our street was Mrs Forde's shop which was next door to our house and was the last house in the terrace. Although it was a relatively small shop it was well stocked with groceries and confectionery and an assortment of goods ranging from paraffin oil to woodbines. Of particular interest to her juvenile customers was a great selection of glass jars on the counter which contained a tempting array of can sweets, bulls eyes, conversation lozenges, toffees at 6 a penny and Lemons Pure Sweets. Adequate supplies of liquorice pipes and Allsorts, Cough-no-Mores, Cleeves slab toffee, and Sticks of Rock were also available. I was often attracted by the daily arrival of Garvey's or Cloran's bakery vans as they delivered fresh bread to Mrs Forde. Cloran's van was still horse-drawn at that time. Other less frequent arrivals were Cleeves' of Limerick and Silke's wholesalers Galway. I got to know the regular van drivers and would hold a watching brief as they sorted their goods in advance of delivery. They say curiosity killed the cat and one day, possibly in an attempt to get rid of me, the driver of Silke's van asked me to do a message for him. Another customer of his had a similar shop around the corner from Church View. I was instructed to go back to Kathleen Fahy's shop on the Galway Road and ask her for the loan of a glass hammer and to enquire if she had any rubber nails. I felt very important to be entrusted with such an important task as I left on the fool's errand. I realised that Miss Fahy was not impressed when I told her what 'Mr Silke;' wanted and I had to return empty-handed. But I was happy enough when he gave me a small bar of chocolate for my trouble. I imagine that 'Mr Silke' got a piece of Miss Fahy's mind on his next visit to Galway Road.

In addition to St Paul's terrace there were 11 other houses on our side of Church View and several vacant sites through which we were able to gain access to Moran's field. These locations were ideal for games of 'Hide-and-go-seek' and 'Cowboys and Indians' and were commandeered for battle when the occasion demanded by the gangs and groupings which we formed. They had names such as 'Mikes' and 'Janies' by which we identified them. Those were, presumably, the names of previous occupiers who were no longer around to hinder our passage. 'Janies', which later became the entrance to the Livestock Mart, was the main unofficial access route to Moran's field. At that time it was overgrown with brambles and nettles and undergrowth of all kinds through which we had beaten paths in the course of our play. Nettle stings were an occupational hazard and were treated by rubbing a wet dock leaf on the affected area. In the absence of a ready water supply a spit was used to dampen the dock leaf. Overgrown clumps of thistles provided us with 'stickers' which we used as ammunition in our boyhood battles as they clung easily to knitted jumpers which were standard items of apparel at the time.

Moran's Field was the main venue for football and hurling which were strictly boys only activities. When playing football the boys used a method of selecting teams which we called 'bulyam' and 'thigum'. Two members of the group would put themselves forward as rival captains. These were generally the biggest or best players or the more assertive ones. 'Bulyam' would have first choice and 'Thigum' would have second choice and they would continue choosing alternately until all available members were selected. Those perceived to be the best were chosen early but hope sprang eternally from the remaining warriors as they awaited selection. It was quite a good lesson in humility, something I can vouch for, to make a team as 'Thigum's' last choice but there was no sentiment shown on such occasions. I believe those terms came from the Irish words *buailim* and *tuigim*. I am assured by a friend of mine from the Joyce Country that in that region when laying down a challenge it was common for a person to use the phrase *buailim ort* and the person accepting the challenge would respond with *tuigim leat*. It is interesting that the phonetic versions of those words found their way into the street games of town children. Another friend of mine tells me that those same words were in use in Co. Sligo in his childhood. Many other Irish words were common in the everyday vernacular of Tuam in our childhood.

When Moran's field wasn't available due to the threatening approach of Tom Moran, the owner, we resorted to playing on the street. We would have to move onto the footpath when a motor car or lorry made an appearance or when O'Connors' cows were being driven home for their evening milking. Matches had to be abandoned when the pitch became unplayable if the homeward, well-fed herd left a carpet of *cac bó* in its wake and we had to wait until the next shower of rain arrived to clear the decks. These hazards were accepted as part of the natural order of things and perhaps, subconsciously, prepared us to tolerate greater inconveniences which we would later encounter on the road of life. The *Léana* field back the Weir Road was another venue for football where we joined the Claureen and Galway Road contingents for matches. I remember one year when the field got seriously flooded after an intense period of rain, instead of playing football in it we swam there in the lukewarm rain waters until the flood eventually subsided and normal business resumed. It seems that the field was reverting to its natural state as the word *léana* is the Irish for 'a low lying grassy place' or 'water-meadow'. Collecting for a football at that time was an old, local tradition and a major undertaking which took us well beyond our own territory before there was enough in the kitty for the purchase. The various factions combined for this purpose and there were occasional rows as to who would be the keeper of the precious leather after the ball was purchased. When hurling on the street we used a sponge ball instead of the usual *sliotar* (or hurling ball) and one had to be careful not to cause damage to the windows and front walls, or to encroach into the flower beds in the front gardens, of houses in the firing line. There was always the temptation to let fly at the hopping ball and hope that it wouldn't be canted over a low-lying house top. Confiscation of the offending missile was regularly threatened by the offended householder but seldom carried out.

There were approximately 20 houses on the opposite side of Church View most of which backed onto O'Connors' field. Some of those houses were thatched houses which had come to the end of their long and eventful lives. In some cases the owners built new houses in the gardens behind the old houses and I can recall several occasions when we enjoyed the spectacle of a bonfire as the thatch on an old house was set on fire before the house was demolished and the space cleared to become the front garden of the new house. Some residents of the street moved to the new houses which had recently been erected by the local authority on Gilmartin Road, which was named after the Archbishop of the time, leaving their old homes to eventually become vacant sites. I remember one lady who lived alone and who was allocated one of the new houses. On the day she left Church View all available hands were employed to carry out the evacuation. Her belongings were piled high in a handcart which was pushed by some of the older boys and young men to her new house. Even the smaller children were enlisted to transport her more fragile possessions. I was entrusted with the picture of the Sacred Heart which had hung over her mantelpiece for a lifetime and warned to make sure that I didn't break the glass. I can still recall the excitement of that exodus from Church View, proceeding around the corner along Cloonthue Road, also known as Tierboy Road in our childhood, and delivering the precious cargo, intact, at the front door of Bridget Curley's new house on Gilmartin Road. I was rewarded with a Kerry Cream biscuit for my efforts. Without realising it, we were witnessing a fundamental changing of the old order in Church View.

The *Cúlán* was the venue for much of our youthful activity. Its entry point was between Mc Kenna's house and where Mrs Forde's shop was located before she moved across the street to St Paul's Terrace. The Hardimans later built a new house in that location. The *Cúlán* gave us access to an area at the rear of the houses which was a sort of commonage at the time and which adjoined O'Connor's field. During the summer holidays we would spend hours digging holes in the ground until they were deep enough for us to use them as hideouts. We would then cover them over with old pieces of timber or linoleum or galvanised iron. Arguments over territory would sometimes cause splinter groups to set about digging their own hideout. I remember on more than one occasion being on the receiving end of a skirmish when a dissatisfied 'rebel' rained stones down on our galvanised roof causing us to abandon our post. We spent many happy summer days in the *Cúlán* in this way. But life was not all sunshine and I recall vividly a day when tragedy entered our boyhood world.

Two boys were playing in the ruins of an old house in a place we used to call 'the porch' which at that time was an entry into the other end of the *Cúlán* from the Cloonthue Road. They were apparently prising stones from the gable end of the old house when a portion of the wall fell and trapped one of them beneath it, fatally injuring him. When we heard the rumbling sound of the falling wall we ran to the scene and observed the frantic efforts of several adults to rescue the trapped boy. I have never forgotten that day and some years ago I wrote the following lines about that particular incident:

The Cúlán.

In memory of Frank Lohan.

Up the *Cúlán* we played cowboys and hide-and-go-seek.
Hedges and holes, hollowed in the ground, our hiding places.
The gable-end of a ruined house our Alamo.

Two boys hacked mortar from its weather-beaten wall.
We ran from our hideouts when we heard the crumbling sound.
Young Frank was pinned beneath the fallen stones.

Big John Halligan strained to lift the fatal slab.
Mrs. Dillon held a mirror to his handsome face.
No misting on the glass to signal hope.

His frantic father came running, stumbling over the furrowed field.
Tearful women gathered round him bewailing his lovely ladeen.
Calvary came to the *Cúlán* on that summer Saturday.

On Sunday they laid him out in his snow-white confirmation shirt.
He wore the medal won for sprinting at the school sports
in springtime.
Its silver sparkled in the light of the blessed candle.

My Mother and my sister Eileen on the prom in Galway

My sisters Noreen and Eileen with Mattie Murphy

6. People on the Move

It was a time when streets were pedestrian friendly and well populated. There always seemed to be people on the street, walking on the footpath or on the road, cycling, driving ass carts and horse carts and floats to and from the town and the station. The busiest times were Sundays when people were going to and coming from Mass and Saturdays when people were going to the market with carts laden with farm produce. We got to know the regular passers-by and greetings were exchanged between them and the locals as everybody seemed to know one another. 'God Bless the work, Mick' would be a common salute if my father was outside working in the front garden. 'You too, Tom (or Dick or Harry)' would be his automatic response.

People coming into town from the Galway Road or the Weir Road had a choice of going by the Claureen and on through High Street or coming up through Church View and on by Vicar Street. All funerals came by Church View, usually in the evening time. I remember being surprised to see a funeral passing through one morning while on my way to school at around 9 a.m. with an unusually large number of cars following the hearse. The only local person I recognised in the cortege was Dr Tom Costelloe. The funeral was that of William Butler Yeats, the poet, on its way to Sligo for burial. He had died several years earlier in France and because of the war there was a delay in returning his remains to Ireland until they had been landed at Galway port early that morning.

There were few cars on the streets during the war years except on the days of the Galway races when they would come out of storage for the occasion. We took the registration numbers of the cars passing through the street on their way to Galway and vied with one another as to who would have the most numbers at the end of the day. There were many regular passers-by whom we got to know well. These included men who came in from the Sylane and Woodquay area with carts of turf which they sold in the *Seamlas*. Another popular arrival was a man who came in from the Headford area for the Saturday markets as he brought a cart load of scollops (from the Irish word *scolb*) which were used for thatching but which were occasionally pilfered from their bundles by the more daring chaps as he passed up through Church View. They were used for a variety of purposes. They were ideal for 'sword-fighting' which we would engage in after watching the Three Musketeers or Erroll Flynn at the matinees in the Mall Cinema. Full length scollops were used to try to hit the bats which used to fly under the street lamp opposite the *Cúlán* on dark nights.

Shorter versions of the scollop were used to bowl hoops or to play 'chinny' a game we played regularly on the street. That game required a small stick which was pointed at both ends and a length of scollop was used to strike one end of the stick, tip it up and strike it again before it reached the ground. Turns were taken at striking the pointed stick until one player missed and then it became the turn of the next player. I believe the game of 'chinny' was a form of hurling. The word comes from Scots Gaelic and is related to the game of shinty which is the Scottish equivalent of hurling.

Neddy Owens, the town crier, would attract our attention as he did his rounds of the town streets ringing his bell to announce the forthcoming arrival of Duffy's Circus to Halligan's field around the corner in the Claureen or the more frequent, but important, news that the water from the town supply was going to be cut off. It seems that leaking pipes were a common cause of those disruptions in those

forties when emigration was a relentless reality and people came to the station in groups to 'see off' their loved ones. To us they were just events in the natural scheme of things and as mere spectators we would not have understood fully the emotions of those for whom the partings were so painful. However we could always enter into the spirit of the joyful homecomings of those returning at Christmas and other holiday times when the journeys were reversed.

On fair days, especially during school holidays, we would watch cattle being loaded into wagons bound for the North Wall and I often stood with other children on top of the railway footbridge near the station gates as the steam engines shunted underneath. When we waved the fireman would blow-off a cloud of steam in which we would be temporarily engulfed. On a few occasions I got a spin on the engine of a train going to the Beet Factory siding a mile or so away. We knew all of the men who worked at the station and they knew us. There always seemed to be a great sense of camaraderie and friendship among those men which filtered through to us children. Many of the families living in the immediate vicinity of the station were 'railway' families and formed a sort of community within a community. We were as familiar with the comings and goings of the other railwaymen as we were with our own fathers and knew them not just by their names but by the nicknames which were used by their colleagues to distinguish them from one another. If they were close acquaintances or work colleagues their exchange would be prefaced by the greeting 'ah the lashin' man', a phrase which I think was in common usage among railway men.

The railway, like the Beet Factory, was an important source of employment in those years employing a large number of people in its various sections. The station was a busy place especially during the beet campaigns which generally overlapped with the Christmas period with 'specials' of beet passing through at all times of the day and night from the beet growing areas of south Galway and the midlands. It was the era of steam and Tuam was an important locomotive depot at that time. Each year during the beet campaign there were additions to the local complement of railwaymen from other railway towns, such as Athlone, where there were also locomotive depots. We got to know those men through their annual visits as they lodged in various houses in the vicinity. Their working hours, like my own father's, were long and varied and would be classed as 'unsocial' in the modern era.

In addition to the wagon loads of beet passing through to the Beet Factory, the area around the station, where the new road is now located, would be filled with lorries loaded with beet which was collected from farmers in the Tuam hinterland and the tillage areas of south Mayo and Roscommon. The lorries were parked there in readiness for delivery to the

Railway Men:

Robert Foster, Sammy Symington, Paddy Reidy, Paddy Cassidy, Ned O'Brien, Joe Connolly, Jimmy O'Meara

factory on the following day. When they had delivered their loads they would fill up with pulp for distribution to the farmers who had supplied the beet. The distinctive aroma of beet pulp would fill the air around the station and town. When mingled with the smell of turf smoke, it was a uniquely aromatic feature of the Tuam of our childhood.

My Father

Next to the railway station was Egan's Mineral Water factory which, like the railway, was an important source of employment in Tuam at that time. During the war years there was a charcoal burning operation carried on in a nearby house as some of Egan's lorries were fitted with a charcoal burning apparatus because of the scarcity of petrol. Opposite the Mineral Water Factory was Moran's garage which was the main dealer for Ford Motors and was an important source of employment. At that time there was a busy saw-mill attached to the garage and the large tree trunks were stored in Moran's field before being cut into timber planks. Consequently there was always a plentiful supply of sawdust available for jumping into from the tree trunks. Old cars from the garage were also parked nearby and they were also a great source of diversion for the young lads from the area. We spent many hours climbing over the tree trunks, diving into the adjacent heaps of sawdust and 'driving' derelict cars on imaginary escapades.

There were regular opportunities in Church View to attract the attention of curious, adventurous teenagers with time on their hands. At one stage there was a slaughter house at the back of Leahy's house on our side of the street where I often joined with Junior Leahy in 'assisting' his cousin, Brod Kedward, who had a butcher shop up town, at the business of slaughtering cattle and sheep. We would barely flinch when he pole-axed a beast or gave the knife to a sheep's jugular but a man's work in those days was not for the squeamish or faint-hearted. His brother, Basil Kedward, who was an international boxer, lived in Church View for a period and did some of his training there. He had a punch bag which he used to allow John Noel Ryan and myself use and occasionally supplied us with boxing gloves whilst trying to teach us some of the finer points of the noble art of self-defence. He soon realised that he was wasting his time as John Noel and I were more interested in swapping comics than swapping punches.

7. A Season for Everything

Autumn was the time of year when chestnuts ripened and we would go into the Deanery on the way home from school to collect a supply for playing 'conkers'. The more of your opponent's chestnuts you could break with your own one the more prestigious you became. For every chestnut of an opponent smashed you acquired an additional degree of 'horsepower' for your own one. Some fellows would put the chestnuts up the chimney to have them well seasoned and hard to break and you would hear fellows boasting of having a '10 horsepower' or maybe a '20 horsepower' one. That was also the time of year when we cycled out to Castlehackett on the slopes of Knockma or out the Dunmore Road to Park Rua to gather hazel nuts to have a good supply for Hallow E'en. On that night we played snap-apple and ducked our heads in a basin of water to try and retrieve coins placed in the bottom of the basin. Both of those games were supposed to be played without using one's hands but inevitably there would be a certain amount of cheating leading to rows in a crowded household.

It was also the time for harvesting apples. There are few sights more pleasing to the eye than a tree laden with ripe apples. A particular treat for us when we served mass was when the Archbishop's housekeeper recruited some of us to pick the apples in the garden attached to his residence. Our reward was that each of us would get a bag of apples. We used our mass-servers duffel bags to bring the booty home. Raiding orchards was an activity which only the more adventurous fellows attempted. The risk of being caught was enough to deter the faint hearted.

Another name that we had for Hallow E'en was *búdán* night. This got its name from a 'game' indulged in by some of the older and more daring chaps but seriously frowned on by the adults. A *búdán* (pronounced boodhawn) was a large cabbage stalk. There was always a plentiful supply of them in the back gardens after the summer crop of cabbages had been used up. They were collected in bundles and used as ammunition, the targets being the front doors of the houses on the street. They made an almighty wallop against a wooden door but did little damage other than leaving a trail of clay from the roots which would be still attached to them. The trick was to have disappeared out of sight and out of reach before the irate householder came on the scene or else there would be dire consequences.

In winter we looked forward to the first signs of frost so that we could make slides. In our case the main slide was situated under the light of the street lamp opposite the *Cúlán*. All we needed was a bucket of water which was thrown on the road and a few of the bigger lads with hobnailed boots would soon have a slide started. As it got longer and slippier more clients were attracted to it, including casual passers-by, and there would often be a queue waiting to take turns on the slide. It could become hazardous at times when the heavyweights took over and could even degenerate into hunker sliding, a practice which was frowned upon by the more orthodox participants because it could result in a serious fall if the hunkered one crashed into someone from behind and took the legs from under him. The term 'hunker-slider' made its way into the local vernacular when referring to someone who was a devious operator. And if someone was referred to as 'a proper hunker-slider' you knew that he was a *persona non grata*, as far as the speaker was concerned, and one to be wary of.

If there was a fall of snow it would be considered a bonus as snowball fights were very popular and brought a welcome level of excitement onto the scene. Certainly there was no lack of physical activity in our lives and the term 'child obesity' hadn't been invented yet. The main hazards of the time were chilblains which were caused by getting ones feet and hands wet and *oighearach* (eyeruck) which was caused by the chafing of the skin above the knees by the leg ends of the short pants worn by boys until they were into their teens.

As well as games there were various customs which were a feature of the times. On New Year's eve we went around with the lantern. There used to be nice coloured paper Chinese lanterns available, in the shape of an upturned concertina, into which we would insert small candles like those used nowadays on birthday cakes. In the event that no lantern was available turnips would be hollowed out and faces cut in the sides so that the light would shine through the holes. We would go from door to door, sometimes getting a penny or two or maybe a biscuit or sweet. The excitement was in the preparation and in the participation in what was an annual event rather than in the results achieved.

On the 1st February there was the custom of going around with the *brídeog* to commemorate the feast of St Bridget. A small container such as a cardboard shoe box stuffed with hay or straw was used containing a doll or a small effigy which represented a child. Sometimes a small sod of turf wrapped in a newspaper is all that would be available.

At Christmas time we went around 'with the mummers'. This involved dressing up in all sorts of gear and going from house to house singing and collecting money, if we were lucky enough. This was generally orchestrated by the bigger girls and all the small kids would be recruited to make up the numbers and dressed in all sorts of exotic costumes. I remember being dressed from head to toe by Baby O'Brien who used her mother's lace curtains for the occasion. It was before the era of face painting as we now know it but boot polish and crayons were lavishly applied to hide our identities as we ventured forth.

On St Stephen's day the bigger lads would go 'around with wren' (pronounced 'ran' in Tuam). At each house they would call out the traditional rhyme

The wren, the wren, the king of all birds,
St Stephen's day was caught in the furze,
Up with the kettle, down with the pan,
Give us a penny to bury the wren.'

Also there was a custom of 'going around with the waits'. This activity took place late at night or in the early hours of the morning in the days leading up to Christmas when people were already in bed. It involved a few men going through the streets during the night calling out the names of the various householders and family members as they passed each house and wishing them a Happy Christmas. I remember hearing them when I was young. The term 'waits' was an early medieval name for a watchman and derived from the Old Norman-French *waite*. The name applied specifically to a watchman in either a fortified place or a town. They stood watch over the castles at night when nobody else was allowed abroad. The role of the Waits moved from the castles to the towns and every medieval town had its own band of musicians who were called the Waits. They were supplied with high-pitched pipes which were similar to the modern oboe. These pipes became known as 'Waits Pipes' and were first used to sound alarms to alert the townspeople to any danger. The duties of the Waits varied from time to time and place to place, but included playing their instruments through the town at night, waking the townsfolk on dark winter mornings by playing under their windows. The formal role of the waits was abolished in the 19th century though the name lingered on as Christmas Waits, who could be any group of singers or musicians who formed a band in order to sing and play carols for money around their town or village at night over the Christmas period.

The custom had obviously found its way into Irish towns like Tuam, by the 20th century. I think the last practitioners of this custom in Tuam were Bill Heneghan from Barrack St and the famous Packy ('Was I') Reilly one of Tuam's best known characters, whose fame was partly related to the fact that he was the self-appointed, unofficial mascot of the Galway football team during their halcyon days after winning the 1938 All-Ireland. Together the duo would patrol the streets in the small hours of the morning during the pre-Christmas period calling out the names of the householders ('Good night Mr Kelly and Mrs Kelly and all the little Kelly's') and wishing them a Happy Christmas and a prosperous New Year. I believe that in earlier times they would have been accompanied by a musician or two but they were eventually left to their own devices and relied totally on their vocal attributes. It was dying out as a serious cultural activity in our era and it seems that 'Was-I' and company were flogging a dead horse. However it was an annual opportunity for him to augment his ever-precarious financial situation. They would follow up their nocturnal performances in the following days during daylight hours in the areas they had visited to collect donations for their unique contribution to the cultural life of the town.

As our horizons extended beyond the street, 'up town', with all its attractions became an extension of our hunting grounds. Childhood games diminished in their importance and the confines of the street were gradually abandoned as we became involved in other activities more in keeping with a new found freedom and a widening circle of friends.

Pioneer Hall

Dermot Forde, P.J. Monaghan, Billy Leahy and Sean Higgins up the Dublin Road

8. Bells, Books and Candles

As the church was a major focal point in our lives, and being a natural volunteer, I became a member of the mass serving fraternity as soon as I got a chance. Recruitment to the ranks of the servers did not normally happen until third class was reached when Brother Brick, the Superior at that time who taught in the Secondary school, would recruit and tutor newcomers in the Latin responses. My older brother Miko, and his pal Gus Cunningham were fully fledged acolytes by the time I reached the Brothers and had become regular helpers for the cathedral clerk, Miko Holian. They were involved in all sorts of extra-curricular duties such as ringing bells, filling candelabras, putting out banners for the sodalities and helping Ned Gallagher to keep the furnace going during cold weather. On occasions they were entrusted with the task of locking up the cathedral at night time, including the big iron gates at the bottom of the chapel road, if Miko Holian wanted to go to the pictures in the Mall or the Odeon. Those gates were closed each night after 9 p.m. until they were eventually removed when the area in front of the cathedral was opened up. The old Pioneer Hall, where we learned how to play snooker under the watchful eye of Christy Murphy from Foster Row, was demolished at the time as part of that development. One of the large pillars which supported the 'chapel' gates is still standing at the turn into town.

Although I was only in 2nd class and ineligible to be an 'official' server I often hung around with them in their various capacities to the extent that I would have been able to carry out most of the tasks on my own if I was ever allowed to do so. I had quickly learned the Latin responses from listening to the real servers repeating them over and over again in the boys' sacristy where Miko Holian would set up an improvised altar and would go through the motions of 'saying mass' even to the extent of being able to do a good impersonation of Fr Killeen, the Administrator. He occasionaly allowed me to serve on the high altar when there would be a full complement of servers among whom I could be safely absorbed as I had not yet been officially approved by Brother Brick. I would be given what, in agricultural parlance, is called a 'hind-teat' role in the team on such occasions which meant I was never let do any individual tasks but I could hold my own with the best of them when it came to rattling off the Latin responses.

I remember an occasion, I think it was Easter Monday in 1942, when I got the opportunity to perform on my own. It being a bank holiday, the late afternoon streets were quiet as I made my way, full of importance, to the Cathedral, to ring the Angelus bell. It would be the first time that I had carried out this important ritual unaccompanied. The previous week had been a busy one when all the priests of the diocese converged on the Cathedral for the annual Holy Week ceremonies which were such a feature of church life in those days. However no operational responsibilities had been delegated to me during that week as the senior members of the team had pulled rank and jealously guarded their own territories. At this stage I was fully conversant with the bell-ringing protocols required on the various liturgical occasions. I had participated many times, under close supervision, in the tolling of the dead bell, a succession of lonely peals interspersed with a substantially respectful pause. I was *au fait* with the bells announcing Sunday mass times - the extended tolling of the first bell 25 minutes before the appointed time and the short lived last bell which provided tardy late-comers with their final call to worship. Other special occasions required variations on these themes when liberties were taken by some of the bigger fellows who swung on the bell rope and rang what were called 'doublers' until such musical virtuosity was eventually banned. Ringing the *Angelus* was the plum job especially for fresh and ambitious bell-ringers.

The circumstances which led to my imminent engagement were complicated. Easter Monday happened to be the day when the annual races were held in Milltown. The Milltown Races were a big event in the western sporting calendar of the early 1940's. All human life of the local variety descended on that venue including many of the male population of our town and quite a number of the female ones as well. Most of them availed of the special excursion for the occasion from the local railway station. Among those who had departed for Milltown were my older brother and his pal who had found themselves in a serious quandary earlier in the day.

In the morning they had been requisitioned to serve the nuptial mass at the wedding of a local businessman who was marrying a local teacher. Such an engagement was always seen as a real perk and the right-hand men were always given first preference. Weddings which involved nuptial mass were always held at 7 a.m. in the morning and as there were no weddings performed during Lent, Easter Monday was always a popular date for such events. They had each been given a half-crown for their early morning exertions and decided that they would head for the races on the strength of their windfalls. The only snag was that Miko Holian, the sacristan, also made his annual pilgrimage to the race track on Easter Monday and after mass that morning had delegated to two of his favoured helpers the task of ringing the Angelus at six o'clock that evening in his absence. In the normal course of events I would not have been considered up to such an onerous task but as the saying goes 'when all fruit fails, welcome haws'. I was begrudgingly deputed to stand in and was made to feel that I was on trial and likely to be excluded from any further opportunities if I failed to do justice to the task.

As I approached the Cathedral I was conscious of the heavy responsibility that lay on my shoulders. I made sure that I was in good time and carefully climbed the winding stone stairs to the belfry high up in the tower from where you could view the surrounding countryside through the wooden slatted windows. Eventually the clock on the tower chimed six o'clock and after a suitable interval I launched into the business of the day. Three peals at 10 second intervals, then a longer pause and then two more sets of three peals before the home straight of nine peals in succession. I had the whole ritual off to a tee and with great relief I listened to the fading echoes of the bell as I descended the belfry stairs. When I opened the door to the porch of the church I got a fright. Standing there waiting anxiously was Fr Killeen, the Administrator. He said nothing until he realised that there was nobody else coming down from the belfry.

'Was it you that rang the Angelus?' he said with a serious look on his face. Certain that I must have done something seriously wrong I pleaded guilty. After a short pause he said: 'Do you know how to prepare the table for a wedding?' Having been an avid observer of all the rituals which had taken place over the past year I ventured a tentative 'Yes, Father'. 'Well, will you go in and get it ready as there is a wedding on in a few minutes' he said.

I duly proceeded to the boys' sacristy and carried out a small wooden table and placed it inside the altar rails in front of the high altar. There was nobody in the church to observe my nervous performance. I then got a white linen cloth from a large drawer in a press at the back of the altar and laid it out neatly on the table. Next up were the two large brass candlesticks and then the holy water container which I filled from the stone font located inside the side door. Finally I brought a lighted candle from a candelabra to light the candles on the table. All was in readiness when Fr Killeen emerged from the priest's sacristy in full regalia. He carried a large prayer book and wore a black biretta. He was followed by four people, two men and two women. The full wedding party consisted of the bride and groom, the best man and the bridesmaid. The only others present were Fr Killeen and myself. The wedding party moved outside the altar rails and took up their positions in front of the table. Fr Killeen removed his biretta and handed it to me and I stood by with the holy water at the ready.

The ceremony was over very quickly and as I handed Fr Killeen his biretta he told me to put everything back where I got it and to wait outside the sacristy door when I was finished. He went to the priests' sacristy accompanied by the four people where, presumably, the register was signed. When I had put everything away I departed through the servers' sacristy and went around the back of the Cathedral to wait outside the priest's sacristy door as instructed.

In a corner at the rear of the Cathedral I noticed four bicycles parked against the wall. Shortly afterwards the wedding party emerged. To my surprise, the groom came over to me and handed me a red, ten-shilling note saying 'Good man yerself'. The two women mounted their bicycles and rode off together down the chapel road, turned right and headed out the Dunmore Road. The two men retrieved their bikes and walked leisurely together down the road wheeling the bikes and took a left-hand turning into the town. I presume they adjourned to partake of some liquid encouragement before facing the long road which lay ahead. At the time I didn't give it any thought as I was still too excited with the acquisition of a ten-shilling note.

I waited patiently, as instructed, until Fr Killeen came out. He didn't look as serious this time and he came over and asked me what class I was in. 'Second class, Father', I replied. He then asked me how it came about that I was ringing the Angelus and I told him the circumstances which gave rise to it. I then showed him the ten-shilling note saying: 'the man gave me this. What'll I do with it?' I think I detected the trace of a smile as he said, 'Keep it, and make sure you don't give it to anybody else!' Greatly relieved I took off home in high spirits where my mother had listened anxiously as the sounds of my maiden public musical performance had wafted over the open airways in the quiet evening calm.

'How did you manage?', she asked when I arrived home and assuring her that I had got on well, I informed her that I had assisted Fr Killeen at a wedding. 'At this hour of the day', said she, in slight disbelief. I confirmed that it was the case with the assurance of one who saw nothing at all unusual in what had taken place. I was further questioned as to whether there was a large crowd at the ceremony and informed her that there were only four people at the wedding, two men and two women. She asked me if I knew them and I said no but I thought they were rich people because the man gave me a ten-shilling note. She sat down as I produced the evidence from my pocket and showed it to her. 'I'd better mind that for you', she said, thoughtfully, as she took the proffered note into her safe keeping. I knew, instinctively, that Fr Killeen's advice not to give it to anyone didn't apply to mothers.

Later on, a neighbour friend came in and inevitably the conversation turned to weddings. The neighbour talked knowledgeably about the high profile wedding which had taken place in the early morning. It came as something of a surprise to her when my mother told her that there had been a second wedding that day. I was interrogated in depth with a view to establishing the identity of the pair who had passed unnoticed into the marital state. Trying to be as helpful as possible and after further cross-examination which included questions as to what they were wearing, I remembered a word which I had heard my older siblings using when describing a new suit that a local chap had acquired recently. 'The man was wearing a pinfeather suit' I blurted out. I knew from the laughter of the two women that I had got it badly wrong especially when I heard my mother saying, 'Well he staggered it at least!' I had got my feathers and stripes confused. I was rescued from further cross-examination by the return of the race-goers.

The first question I was asked by my brother was if I had rung the Angelus. Assuring him that the mission had been accomplished successfully I then told him about the ten bob note. He didn't believe me until his mother confirmed that I was telling the truth. He was quiet for a while and gradually adopted a friendlier than usual attitude. In a roundabout way he pointed out that if he hadn't given me the job I wouldn't have come into such riches and went so far as to generously offer to split it with me. After all, five shillings was still a good return for the small task that he had asked me to carry out. I may have been innocent but I wasn't stupid and resisted all his blandishments pointing out that Fr, Killeen said I wasn't to give it to anyone else. He later brought the pal around and they tried the old pals act. By now my share would have been three and fourpence if they had their way but I held firm in the knowledge that I had serious clerical approval for my stand.

The next day they made further overtures and even invited me along to help them with some chores which the sacristan had allocated to them. It was a form of trap because as soon as the sacristan came on the scene they told him what had happened. It was clear to me that the man was quite taken aback at the news as the amount involved was probably more than he would get himself in the normal course of such events. By now it was being suggested by the three other parties involved that a four-way split would be acceptable and that this would give me equal status with them. After all, it was suggested, a half-crown was still a lot of money. I didn't give in and played my trump card when

I said that I had given it to my mother anyway. They knew that they had lost the battle at this point and proceeded to sulk while giving me the cold shoulder.

The following Saturday my mother brought me with her on her weekly shopping expedition down town. We went into O'Malley's Boot and Shoe Store and she helped me try on several pairs of sandals before settling for a pair that fitted well, with adequate room for future expansion. The shop assistant wrapped the shoe box in brown paper and tied it neatly, leaving enough twine to make a double loop which made it easy to carry. After the usual bargaining interlude, he gave my mother sixpence change from the red ten shilling note which she had tendered. She told me to bring the sandals home with me and to remember that they were for Sundays and school and that under no circumstances was I to wear them playing football. She then gave me the precious little silver coin, with its greyhound emblem, which she had received in change and told me that it was for myself. I was now the proud owner of a new pair of brown, leather sandals with crepe soles and a silver buckle on the side. On the way home I went into Michael Lardner's and bought a 'tuppenny' ice-cream wafer and, for later delectation, bought two squares of Cleeves' slab toffee for a penny. I then crossed the Square and went into Byrnes' newsagents where I purchased the latest edition of the 'Dandy' for three pence. When you were in second class in the 1940's, happiness was a well spent tanner!

As a newcomer to the ranks of the mass servers I was always anxious to please and avail of any opportunities that came my way. Having served my time as a useful sub I was eventually accepted into the official complement of servers by Brother Brick who, as well as tutoring the servers, delegated their duties each week. In the pre-Vatican 2 era, servers had a much bigger role to play in the liturgy than is now the case. As well as striking the gong and ringing the bells, the server had to carry the paten at communion time and change the large mass book from one side of the altar to the other before the Gospel reading. Normally the senior members of the team would carry out those tasks. Brother Brick had the habit of rostering the senior fellows for last mass on Sundays, thereby cramping the style of those who wanted to be playing football or pursuing other interests at that time of day. On occasions the smaller fry would be cajoled into standing in for those appointed to duties which didn't fit in with their other social demands and on one such occasion George Lyons and I were serving last mass and delighted to have an opportunity to do the important jobs. When it was time to change the book I approached the altar and had to reach up high to lift the stand as I was just about the height of the altar at the time. The book was quite heavy and the large stand on which it rested was even heavier. As I lifted it off, the large, open book slipped off the stand and fell with a loud bang which reverberated around the cathedral. My father was in the congregation and an elderly man kneeling beside him who was 'nodding off' at the time started up with a groan when he heard the noise. My father must have been greatly embarrassed but not as much as I was especially when, much to my annoyance, George Lyons succeeded in completing the task successfully and without any difficulty. Later on I experienced what could be termed a conflict of interest inasmuch as I joined the Cathedral choir and as it was not possible to be in two places at the same time I had to forego my serving activities if choir duties called.

OTS Group outside Cathedral 1942

Included in photograph are the following: Extreme Left, Standing: John Waldron, Stephen Keane (who worked in Clorans), AN Other, John Hession, the Town Sergeant. The priest holding the cross is Fr McEllin and the server in front of him is Tom Leo. Back Row, Right to Left on platform: D.J Murphy and Jack Bray in LDF uniforms, Tommy Joyce, Fr Prendergast and Fr Scahill. Back Row Right to Left on Ground: Frank Walsh, Eddie Cooley, Bernie Shaughnessy, Tom Higgins. The small boy in front left is Pat Waldron and the server beside him is Sylvester Hopkins.

Seated Left to Right: AN Other, Jarlath O'Connell, Mrs Costelloe, Dr Costelloe, Archbishop Walsh, Bill Comerford, Jimmy Glynn (Sen) with Jimmy Glynn (Jun), and far right Martin (Solid) Rooney.

The small boy standing at right is Michael Cooley and the small server whose head is visible between Jarlath O'Connell and Mrs Costelloe is the author.

9. Scholarly Pursuits

My first encounter with the 'Brothers' was in 'The Hut' which housed 2nd Class. It was a fairly large, old wooden building located in a part of the Christian Brothers' garden where all newcomers lingered for a year before moving into the main school building. We were the last class to occupy it, as a new Primary school was being built at the time of our arrival. It opened in 1941 and I remember the day when the exodus from The Hut to the brand new school took place. Our first teacher was a man called D.J. Murphy from Ballygaddy Road who transferred with us to the new school. To celebrate its opening there was a formal ceremony with a Mass celebrated by the Archbishop and attended by all the local dignitaries. There were long sermons and speeches but my main recollection of that day was the singing of Jarlath Daly, a young boy soprano from the Weir Road, who sang *Bless this House*.

When we moved on to 3rd class we had another lay teacher, Paddy Quinn, who was a native of the town and knew where we were all coming from. It was at that stage that homework became a factor in the school curriculum which consisted mainly of 'sums' and 'compositions'. I found one of the latter among my mother's belongings after she died. It was probably for sentimental reasons as much as for its literary merit that she had held on to it. Thereafter it was Christian Brothers all the way until we finished in the primary school. In 4th class we had Brother Quinn, a ginger-haired Kildare man who was very proud of his roots in the 'short-grass' county. He took a great interest in the school senior football team and used to write pen-pictures of the players for the *Tuam Herald* when they were playing in the Connacht Colleges competitions. On one occasion he asked me to deliver his contribution to Jarlath Burke on my way home from school and, stealing a look at it, I recall names like Jackie Mangan and Kevin Connolly and his referring to the corner forward as the 'wily Stockwell'. One day he held a competition in the class to guess which county he was from. Lots of counties were mentioned until eventually I said 'Kildare', which was the correct answer. He seemed very impressed with my knowledge of accents until later on, during the class, it dawned on him that he had given me a letter to post a few days earlier to a Mrs Quinn in Moyvalley, Co Kildare, so he realised that I had been able to put two and two together. I met Brother Quinn almost 50 years later at a function in Tuam when the Brothers were finally departing the town and he spoke with great affection of his time in Tuam when he was just a young man. He remembered going for walks to places like Gardenfield with other young brothers when they might get a shilling from Brother McKenna to buy some sweets on the way, and how he always got good value from the kind people behind the counter, particularly in one shop down the Ballygaddy Road.

He was replaced by Brother Redmond who, I think, was from Tipperary. He played the accordion and gave us our first dramatic experience when he put on a cowboy sketch for one of the school concerts which was held in the old secondary school. My own contribution to the occasion was a rendering of *Home on the Range* with a chorus of 4th class cowboys. I also remember an occasion when we did extracts from the *Pirates of Penzance, tré Ghaeilge*. Although I never had him as a teacher I also remember Brother Doohan, a Clare man, who also taught 4th class around that time. He was a good hurler and footballer and played a few games with the Tuam Stars senior team while he was stationed in Tuam. I always associate him with the snowfall of 1947 when he led the primary school lads in snowball fights with the secondary school pupils. He would have a wheel-barrow filled with snowballs before leading the charge. The playground in the Primary School became a skating rink for weeks and he spent as much time on the slides as his pupils.

Brother Vaughan, a Limerick man, taught us in 5th class. He was big into music and hurling and always extolled the exploits of the great Limerick hurling team of the thirties and early forties. We were very familiar with names such as Mick Mackey, Paddy Clohessy and Jackie Power who were the stars of his favourite team and of that era. He was fastidious in his tastes especially when it came to the month of May when there was competition between the various classes as to which had the best May altar. The month would start in a blaze of colour but as the days passed the supply of flowers would dwindle and the early specimens would begin to wither. On one such occasion he commanded us to bring in fresh supplies even if we had to 'beg, borrow or steal' them. Pupils from places west of the railway gates, such as Church View, would often take a short cut through the Deanery on the way to school and on the day after Brother Vaughan's appeal for fresh supplies one overly anxious individual, on his way to school with a rather pathetic bunch of home grown specimens, was tempted to supplement his contribution with a more healthy looking selection from Dean Jackson's garden which included a generous supply of the master's favourite tulips. I'm sure he hadn't intended to be taken so literally but, after he had neatly arranged the fresh blooms on the altar, nobody would have been able to distinguish the catholic ones from the protestant ones. Reflecting on that incident I would like to think that it represented a sub-conscious ecumenical gesture on the part of the donor and that was long before the issue was brought into the public domain by Vatican Two.

Brother Vaughan was the choirmaster and Fr Scahill, who was

the organist in the Cathedral, came regularly to the school for practice sessions and between them they had us well trained. Brother Vaughan was a perfectionist and didn't suffer fools gladly. On one occasion we were practising the hymn *To Jesus' Heart all Burning* and not performing to his satisfaction. One of the lines in the hymn is *O Heart for me on fire,* and after a number of abortive attempts at getting the correct emphasis on the last word, he sang what turned out to be a mocking imitation of our efforts and ordered us to sing it again. Full of enthusiasm, and feeling fairly sure of myself, I sang it louder than ever putting in three emphatic, short syllables where there should only have been one long one. I got a box on the ear for my effort and literally saw stars. I had taken him up wrongly and, in his frustration, he assumed that I was being cheeky and had been deliberately mocking him. The only thing that was on fire for the rest of that session was my ear and I remained silent in protest for the duration of the class. I think he had second thoughts later on when he saw my reaction and a couple of days later he held a competition in the class for a valuable prize. I don't think it was a coincidence that the subject matter he chose was one of my strong points and I was the proud owner of a brand new hurl on my way home from school that day. All was forgiven, if not forgotten.

The choir consisted of pupils from both the CBS primary and secondary schools. Its main function was to sing at the various ceremonies in the cathedral where we joined with the men's choir. At that time the cathedral choir was all-male, made up of men in the senior choir and boys from the CBS who sang the soprano and alto parts. Believe it or not, women were not allowed into the choir in those days. The only women I ever saw in the organ loft were Miss Walsh from High St who used to play the organ occasionally and Sr Magdalen from the Mercy convent who was organist for the Christmas carols broadcasts. The choir also took to the streets to collect money for the

St Vincent De Paul Society during the Christmas period and brought an air of festivity to the town during the dark nights of winter. I think the carol singing started at Christmas time in 1942 as may be deduced from the following paragraph in the *Tuam Herald* at that time:

> "There was something new in Tuam's Christmas this year, the carol singing. And yet in its newness it was something very old, for carol singing is almost as old as Christmas itself. The carols bring a touch to the festival that is not of this modern, materialistic world. If you have heard the carollers you will realise that it is almost strange to hear in the distance children's sweet voices tinkling like bells in the night ….*Adeste Fideles, Silent Night.* And then to hear the swell of a chorus of male voices in *Cry Out and Shout,* and *How Beautiful upon the Mountains.* Yes, that was the real Christmas. No wonder the householders opened their purse strings wide and gave generously to the St Vincent De Paul Society collectors. It takes more than mere music to do that; it was the spirit in the carols. And how well the singers brought out that spirit. Cold rain or biting wind passed unheeded when the Christmas hymns filled the air. It was a treat and the organisers deserve our thanks. The singing was grand and a credit to the singers and their teachers. It was a welcome innovation to our 1942 Christmas and may it long continue'.

The carol singing became a regular annual event from then on as a notice in the *Herald* the following Christmas indicated that the people of the town would be pleased to hear that the Cathedral Choir had decided to continue the good work and would be performing in the different streets of the town on successive nights culminating each night at 10.30 pm with a recital at the Square.

Brother Vaughan and Fr Scahill were also the driving forces behind the annual Christmas carol service which used to be broadcast on Radio Eireann on a Sunday around Christmas. The *Herald* reported that several new carols would be included in the programme to be broadcast from the Cathedral at Christmas, 1943 and the choir would consist of over 400 children selected from choirs from the CBS, the Mercy and Presentation Convents and St Jarlath's College together with 50 male voices from the Cathedral Choir supplemented by senior pupils from St Jarlath's. Among the new carols on that programme were *Hail Smiling Morn*, *While Shepherd's Watched* and *It Came Upon The Midnight Clear*. The broadcast concluded with the *Hallelujah Chorus* from Handel's *Messiah*. Sr Magdalen from the Mercy convent was the organist on those occasions and combined with Fr Scahill and Brother Vaughan to make this an important annual event in the liturgical calendar of Tuam in the 1940's.

I enjoyed being in the choir and the opportunity it provided to experience at first hand the music of the various liturgies. The *O Salutaris* and the *Tantum Ergo* sung during Benediction and the plain chant *Dies Irae* of the requiem mass still come readily to mind after all those years. On many occasions only a few regulars would turn up, especially during the summer holidays, as the men would be at work. Tom Higgins from the Old Road, a staunch member of the men's choir, would round up any available and willing hands so that Fr Scahill would have a reasonable 'quorum' of singers for the requiem masses. He would sometimes cross our palms with silver in appreciation of the fact that at least we had turned up. At the time we took it for granted without realising what a great experience it was to perform to the accompaniment of an accomplished organist in such a sacred venue. Inevitably boyhood voices break and when my turn came I decided it was time to retire and didn't turn up for choir duty for a couple of weeks. I met Fr Scahill one day and he quizzed me as to why I wasn't turning up to the choir. I told him that my voice had broken and I felt I had to leave. 'As of now you are in the men's choir' he said 'so I want to see you back immediately'. I met Fr Scahill in Galway a few years ago and we reminisced about the times and the people who had featured in the organ loft in Tuam Cathedral in former times and wondered where the years had gone. Ever the mathematician, he informed me that he had then 'become of age' for the fourth time, having reached the age of 84. He and many of his choristers are now part of the heavenly chorus but the echoes of his musical repertoire still linger in the Tuam air.

Brother Mullen was the principal of the Primary school. He taught 6th class and prepared us for our first formal examination, the Primary Certificate, which marked the end of our primary education. My passage through the school doesn't appear to have left too many psychological or other scars but it saddens me to hear stories from time to time of young people whose experiences of school were traumatic and unpleasant. I may have survived through being reasonably diligent and adept at 'toeing the line'. I can only speak for myself but the teachers I encountered were generally decent men who worked hard in difficult times and situations. My time in the primary school more or less coincided with the Second World War years and it would be interesting, if one were so inclined, to examine the educational impact that had on our generation.

What I remember best about those schooldays is the football and hurling after school, the general camaraderie with school pals, the holidays and the many extra mural activities to which I was easily attracted and of course the choir. Those interests made the transition from primary to secondary school fairly seamless. Whilst many of our classmates went in different directions at that point, those of us who remained on in the CBS had only to move across to the old school where we were joined by new blood from the national schools in the town's hinterland for the next phase of our educational journey. Some moved to the Technical School farther up the Dublin Road where they had the opportunity to study subjects which they felt were more relevant to their future career prospects, particularly those who were to take up engineering apprenticeships in the Beet Factory. Some went to St Jarlath's as day pupils, joining up with the large contingent of boarders in what was then an important Diocesan College. Some went to secondary schools elsewhere including several who pursued religious vocations. And others finished with school at different stages during the following years before going into the world of work. As far as I can recall I was one of 56 pupils in 6th class in the Primary School (c1946) and I have a photograph taken in second year in the Secondary school (1948) where only 14 of those appear and only 7 appear in the photos of my Leaving Cert class (1951/2).

There was still a fair amount of overlapping between the primary and secondary school pupils particularly for those involved in sporting and choral activities both of which helped to bridge the gap before boyhood voices broke. After Brother Vaughan was transferred a Brother Murphy took the choir over. At one of the annual concerts which was held in the Odeon Cinema some of us from both schools had to play the part of girls. The attempts at fashion were rather pathetic by modern standards as there was no question of recruiting any real female participants. The only available 'females' were, in the main, decked out in their mothers' or sisters' dresses with a variety of headgear *a la* Carmen Miranda. Brother McKenna was the superior at that time. He had a reputation of being very cultured and accomplished in musical and artistic matters and was a regular exhibitor with people like Jarlath O'Connell and John Henihan in the annual Art Exhibition which used to be held during the Easter vacation in St Jarlath's College. However

Concert Group taken in Tuam CBS Primary School yard on 12th April, 1948

Front Row: Pat Hurley, Noel Manley, Mickey Naughton, Mickey Leo, Danny Hickey, Christy Byrne, Tommy Monahan, Gerry Ferguson, Joseph Moroney, Michael Monaghan. Second Row: Frankie Keane, Martin Quinn, Tommy Kelly, Sonny McNamara, Frank O'Mahoney, Eamonn Moggan, Jarlath Burke, Sean Donnellan, Tommy Murphy, Joe Collins, Mickey Moggan, Andy O'Connell, Frank Naughton, Gerry O'Connor, John Henihan, Noel O'Donoghue, Eddie Rooney, Kevin O'Brien, Jamesy Corbett. Back Row: Gerry King, Michael Moroney, Sean Holian, Raymond O'Donoghue, Gerry Coady, Gay Heskin, Noel Loftus, Leo Flanagan.

he was quite narrow in some of his views. He was particularly critical of jazz which I heard him describing on one occasion as the music of the devil. He was not happy with one of the songs which Brother Murphy had chosen for the concert. It was the only funny song on the list and was sung by Gerry Coady. It went as follows:

'I know a girl who lives down the street

Her name is Eliza, she has two big feet.

Eliza's two feet, Eliza's feet,

There's no mistake, they take the cake, Eliza's two big feet.'

After Brother McKenna attended the dress rehearsal the song was excluded from the programme. Perhaps it was not in the best taste, and that certain 'Elizas' might have taken offence, but it was really a harmless piece of nonsense. It's amazing the things one remembers.

At any rate the concert went on without 'Eliza'. There were some very good singers in that group including Danny Hickey and Christy Byrne who sang *Roses in Picardy*. My own contribution, in the guise of someone called 'Rita,' was a song called *Because* which was difficult enough to sing without having to do so wearing one's mother's dress. It probably wasn't easy to listen to either.

Tommy Kelly, George Lyons and Murt McCormack in the College field

10. Secondary Events

My time in the secondary school was from the mid-1940s to 1952. It was long before the introduction of 'free' education so that class sizes were relatively small by comparison with later times. The regime in the secondary school was quite different from that which we were familiar with in the primary school. Having a half day on Wednesdays for games was a welcome feature initially, but it was cancelled out by having to attend school on Saturday mornings. The concept of evening study was introduced at that stage and the fact that we had to stay in the school for that purpose encroached further on the freedoms previously enjoyed. The curriculum followed was also very different to what became available later, with a lot of the emphasis on the 'humanities' subjects and plenty of time and attention devoted to Christian Doctrine. It reflected the religious and nationalistic ethos of the time and much of what was omitted would have been at least as relevant and interesting as that which was included. History seemed to be mainly about battles long ago and focused on ancient events rather on more recent happenings. For instance there was very little emphasis on the various political movements of the late 19th and early 20th century that culminated in the founding of the new state. There was no mention of the First World War in school nor was there any discussion of our own Civil War even though six young men from the county were executed by a firing squad of fellow Irishmen during that conflict just a few hundred yards from our school. Proper analysis of those issues would have shown the obscenity of all wars. Perhaps it was still too raw and it is claimed by some that such policies ensured that our generation was protected from the divisions created by such conflicts. It could also be claimed that it delayed the healing process created by those divisions which have continued to affect the country up to the present day.

One of the most serious deficiencies at the time, in my opinion, was the absence of any science subjects on the curriculum. Whilst this may have been because of a lack of resources available to schools during and in the aftermath of the war, and in light of the prevailing economic situation, it was disappointing as science had been taught there in earlier years as was evident from the presence of a variety of unused equipment and furnishings in the old science room which we often used for togging out on the way to Parkmore. Leaving aside mathematics, for instance there were no business oriented subjects, such as accounting, taught at that time and the concept of computer studies was unknown. The period of our secondary education was pre television, pre talk-radio and pre computers. When one considers the variety of subjects and the plethora of technological and other supports available to the present generation of scholars the respective educational environments bear little comparison. But we survived.

Having different teachers for the various subjects was a welcome novelty as far as I was concerned exposing us to different styles and personalities and new interests. In first year we had a teacher called Paddy Noone, a Tuam native, who had taught in the school for many years and who used to tell us of events that had happened there 'about forty years ago'. He was the first to introduce us to Shakespeare and by the time we had finished first year we had enough of the *Merchant of Venice* to last a lifetime, including large passages which we learned 'off by heart', a feature which is now referred to as rote learning and appears to be frowned upon in some quarters. Even though I might not be able to recite it now I can still take pleasure in reading Portia's admonition to Shylock regarding the concept of mercy:

'The quality of mercy is not strained.
It droppeth as the gentle rain from heaven
Upon the place beneath. It is twice blest:
It blesseth him that gives and him that takes.
Tis mightiest in the mightiest; it becomes
The throned monarch better than his crown.
His sceptre shows the force of temporal power,
The attribute to awe and majesty,
Wherein doth sit the dread and fear of kings.
But mercy is above this sceptred sway;
It is enthroned in the hearts of kings;
It is an attribute of God himself;
And earthly power doth then show like God's
When mercy seasons justice.'

More than six decades later I can appreciate the depth and significance of such lines much more fully than when Paddy Noone first introduced them to us.

In 2nd year we had a teacher called Sean Lynch who taught English and Latin. He was a very good teacher and a real stickler especially for grammar. In addition to Irish and English a third language was then an essential requirement for those who would need to do the Matriculation exam if going on to university and Latin was the only additional language on the curriculum at that time. As it turned out our ears were fairly well attuned to the sound, as distinct from the meaning, of Latin words from our time as servers of the Latin mass so it didn't sound as foreign as one might have expected. It certainly didn't sound like a foreign language when spoken with a very distinctive Kerry accent. I still have a very dilapidated copy of *Longman's Latin Course* which was his 'bible' as far as that language was concerned and the bane of many lives. My copy was obviously recycled by a more senior pupil

2nd Year Tuam CBS 1948

Back Row: Seamus Harney, Sean Dolan, Odran Walsh, Sean Fahy, Mick Barratt. 2nd Row: Paddy Joe Howard, Murt Burke, Dan McGrath, Sean Heaney, Eamonn Moggan, Kevin Quigley. Front Row: Paddy Joe King, Richard Fahy, Paschal Howard, Gerard Kennedy, Tommy Kelly, Paudie McCabe.

with an entrepreneurial flair, as his name is still to be found underneath the brown paper covering which helped to protect it to some extent. Mr Lynch was also a keen golfer and some of the lads in our class who lived near the golf course used to caddie for him and get a free 'tutorial' as part compensation for their services!

Jack Bray, another native of the town, taught History, Geography, Drawing and Irish at different stages and to various classes on our journey through the secondary school with a commendable degree of tolerance. His explanations of what we were likely to encounter in the real world were the closest we got to any career guidance and his tongue-in-cheek advice to those who were less than enthusiastic about academic matters was to 'buy a big pane of glass'. In other words to open a shop because the way the world was going they were likely to become very successful business men and leave the rest of us in the shade.

Brother Wrafter arrived in Tuam shortly before our class arrived in the secondary school and was still there when I had finished. He was the dominant personality of our era and taught English and Latin to the senior classes. He also oversaw the sporting activities, particularly the organising of the teams which represented the school in the Connacht Colleges football and hurling competitions. He followed a famous Brother Murphy, a Kerryman, who had coached an excellent

2nd Year Hurlers Tuam CBS 1948

Front Row: Sean Heaney (Tullinadaly); Mick Barrett (Ballygaddy Rd.); Sean Dolan (Ballygaddy Rd.); Eamonn Moggan (Galway Rd.); Kevin Quigley (Killalane). 2nd Row: Paddy Joe King (Demense); Richard Fahy (Barnaderg); Paddy Joe Howard (Galway Rd.); Tommy Kelly (Church View); Paschal Howard (Galway Rd.) Back Row: Gerard Kennedy (Graiguecullaire); Seamus Harney (Old Rd.); Dan McGrath (Athenry Rd.); Murt Burke (Bishop St.); Sean Fahy (Shop St.); Paddy O'Callaghan (Vicar St.).

bunch of footballers who figured prominently in Connacht Colleges competitions in the early forties. It was mainly members of the CBS team which represented Tuam Stars when they won the county minor football championship of 1945. The final of that competition was not played until early in 1946 and the only non-CBS player on the team was the one and only Sean Purcell who was a pupil in St Jarlath's College at the time. I would hazard a guess that that was one of the first big occasions on which the future 'Terrible Twins' featured. Another member of that team, who later became a successful publican, claimed that, but for the fact that he emigrated at an early age, the famous duo would have had to settle for being part of the 'Terrible Triplets'. A terrible beauty may have been nipped in the bud. Around that year also

Tuam Minor Team – Galway County Champions 1945

Front Row: Niall Joyce, Junie Loftus, Jim Fehilly, Paddy Igoe, Bill Forde. Back Row: Brother Wrafter, Frank Stockwell, P.J.Grealish (behind), Padraic Woods, Sean Purcell and Joe Wilson (behind), Willie Mannion, Paddy Nolan, Ned Quinn, Tom Ryan (behind), Sean Maloney, Dermot Forde, Cyril Kelly.

two of our heroes, Jackie Mangan and Frank Stockwell, were on the Connacht Colleges football team which defeated Leinster in Parkmore to win the national competition.

Brother Wrafter was a Dubliner and sociable by nature, as reflected in his involvement in the many extra-mural activities in which he participated in the town, including being a member of the committee responsible for the development of the new Tuam Stadium. He could be moody and sarcastic at times and required subtle humouring if one wanted to be included in the travelling contingent for the next out-of-town match especially if one wasn't on the select panel of players. I recall many happy trips to places like Roscommon, Galway and Ballinrobe in Bernie Daly's hackney car to inter-college matches, on one occasion having to sit on the gear lever of an over-crowded vehicle. I would usually justify my intrusion by ensuring that there was a full

Hurling Group in Tuam CBS taken in Parkmore, Tuam, c1947

Back Row: Brother Doohan, Pat Ferguson, Joe Collins, Brendan Ryan, Walter Harney, Eric Traynor, Sean Dolan, Pos Fahy, Christy O'Gara, Mick Barrett, Bill Forde, Brother Bennett. Front Row: Joe McDonagh, Gerry Coady, Peter Burke, Gerry O'Connor, Tommy Kelly, Dominick Browne

complement of jerseys available for the team and that they would be safely stored in the boot of the car on the homeward journey.

More than once I had to act as an umpire when there was no neutral candidate available. On such occasions each team could nominate their own choice of umpire on the basis that the impartiality, or lack of it, was evenly distributed. But it was a thankless chore in an era when there were no nets on the goal posts, few line markings on the field of play and only one umpire at each end. As a result, the decisions of the unfortunate umpire were often disputed and one was subject to abuse from both teams; from the defenders if you allowed a score and from the attackers if you did not. On one occasion my integrity was

CBS HURLERS c1948

Front Row: Gerry Coady, Dan McGrath, Dom Browne, Sean Dolan, Brendan Ryan, Jimmy Heneghan. 2nd Row: Miko Kelly, Padraic Dolan, Bill Forde, Sean Lohan. Back Row: Paddy Higgins, Bill Leo, Walter Harney, Pos Fahy, Peter Burke, Mick Barrett

questioned by the referee when I gave the benefit of the doubt to my own team after a goalmouth scramble on the basis that the ball hadn't crossed the line. As there was no actual line marking, I contended that it was where I considered it should be. The fact that the goalie and several of the defenders were classmates of mine, and that I would have to travel home in the same car with them, had nothing whatsoever to do with my decision.

We had the luxury of travelling by bus on a journey to Athleague on an occasion when the school team played Roscommon CBS in a hurling match. I also succeeded in getting a lift to Loughrea one Sunday with Brother Wrafter and Pádraic Dolan where we joined a bus taking the Connacht Colleges hurling team to Nenagh to play against Munster Colleges in the All-Ireland semi-final. To the best of my knowledge Pádraic Dolan, who played centre field for Connacht that day, was the only Tuam CBS player to have played on a Connacht Colleges hurling team.

During those years an annual school sports was held and several of the more elite CBS athletes went forward to the Connacht Colleges Competition. These included Jack Mangan who won the High Jump and Bill Forde who won the 7lb Shot in the provincial competition and Tom Nicholson who was a fine long-distance runner. So those of us who only made up the numbers had plenty of real heroes to admire. In those years also there was an annual drill display held in Parkmore during the early summer when we were all decked out in white uniforms and performed to the strains of the Army Band from Athlone. The drill displays also included some gymnastics. These involved some spectacular vaulting over a wooden horse by the more athletic and adventurous types who took to the springboard under the guidance of Brother Laffin who, in addition to his knowledge of the wooden horse, was also a very competent maths teacher.

CBS FOOTBALL TEAM 1950

Back Row: Martin Burke, Anthony O'Donoghue, P.J.Donnellan, Frank Doherty, Tom Nicholson, Sean Donnellan. 3rd Row: Paddy Joe King, P.J. Gannon, Peter Burke, Frank Moggan, Peter Kelly, Sean Fahy, Vinny Ryan, Tommy Brosnan. 2nd Row: Peter McHugh, Jimmy Heneghan, Padraic Dolan, Paddy Higgins, Murt Burke. Front: Mick Costelloe, Gay Heskin.

In 1951 there were week-long celebrations to mark the centenary of the arrival of the Christian Brothers in Tuam and the opening of their first school there. The town was decorated with flags and bunting and a special committee of townspeople, mainly past pupils, was set up to organise the various events. On the first Sunday there was a High Mass in the cathedral at which Archbishop Walsh presided with the combined cathedral and CBS choirs; in the afternoon there was a match in the stadium between Galway and Roscommon for the Egan Cup and that night there was a Grand Celebrity Concert in the Odeon cinema which included a choir of 150 voices with local boy soprano, Danny Hickey, as soloist. It also featured a young man from Galway called Paschal Spellman who was described as Ireland's Youngest Comedian. During that week several other events were held in the town including an official presentation in the Town Hall to the superior general of the Christian Brothers who attended the celebrations.

Afterwards there was a parade through the town and a massed Swedish drill display in Parkmore.

Brother Wrafter became the superior after Brother McKenna retired, and in addition to his teaching duties and sporting interests he was very involved in the organisation of all the extramural activities associated with the school. He was still there when I left Tuam a couple of weeks after doing the Leaving Cert in 1952 and I only saw him once again after that. I was working in Cork for a short period in 1962 and one day, in a crowded Patrick Street, I

Drill Display 1950:
T. Murphy and T. Kelly

saw a familiar figure walking towards me. As we were about to pass we made eye contact and both stopped in our tracks. I had recognised him immediately but I could see that he wasn't sure who I was so I just said 'Tuam'. He shook my hand warmly and we chatted away for a while in the busy street as he recalled names and events which came back to him. It was the first time that we had spoken as man to man, as distinct from master to pupil, and he came across to me as a quiet-spoken, gentle man which was surprisingly different from the rather daunting personality that I had associated with our school days. I could see that he remembered Tuam as a place for which he had a great respect and good memories. Our chance encounter was a bit like that of ships that pass in the night except that we had a few minutes of nostalgic reminiscence before continuing our respective journeys on the sea of life, but bound for different ports.

Leaving Cert Tuam CBS 1952

Front Row: Paddy Duddy (Kilbannon), Don Harney (Old Rd.), Mick Costelloe (Kilconly), Frank Doherty (Kilconly); 2nd Row: Tommy Kelly (Church View), Peter McGrath (Kilbannon), Martin Burke (Cluide), Sean Dwyer (Bishop St.), Michael Flanagan (Kilbannon); Back Row: Paddy Byrne (Kilcreevanty), Des Creaven (Belclare), Michael Maher (Ballyglunin), Paddy O'Donoghue (Belclare), Christy O'Gara (Dublin Rd.).

Group photo in Tuam CBS garden 1951

Back Row: J. Roche, T. Kelly, Vinny Higgins, Odran Walsh, Frank Forde, P.J. McGrath, John Behan. Middle Row: Aidan O'Donoghue, Willie Mannion, - Dunleavy (?), Christy O'Gara, Peter Kelly, Peter Burke, Eamonn Moggan, Paddy Joe King; Front Row: Johnny Gormley, Seamus Moloney, Noel Manley.

11. The Lighter Side

During the 1940's the Sunday matinees in the Mall cinema were a major attraction and were the social highlights of our week. It was an achievement to have the four pence required for admission to Patty O'Connor's emporium by the time matinee time arrived. When the Odeon came on stream it was sometimes difficult to choose between the rival establishments. At that time there was a high wall around the Protestant Bishop's palace which was then in Bishop St opposite the chapel gates where Jack Flanagan, the local bill poster, with his bucket and brush, would paste the programme of films for the coming week. It was an object of great interest as we came out from the children's 9 a.m. Sunday mass to find out what was on in the matinee that afternoon. It usually consisted of two films, one a cowboy and the other a comedy with a serial in between which kept us guessing from week to week as to what was going to happen next.

Cowboy pictures were the most popular, our heroes being Hopalong Cassidy, Johnny McBrown and Roy Rogers with supporting characters like Gabby Hayes, Gene Autry and the singing 'Sons of the Pioneers' who provided us with enough material for re-enactment of their exploits for the rest of the week. And of course the tomahawk wielding Indians were always the bad guys. Comedies featuring such characters as Laurel and Hardy, Abbott and Costello and Old Mother Riley were very popular as were The Dead End Kids and The Bowery Boys. We had a great loyalty to the Mall because it had been around longer than the Odeon, which was a relative newcomer to the entertainment scene in Tuam, when we were at the matinee-going stage. I remember when the Odeon opened in 1943 there were queues along Shop St to see *They Died with their Boots On*, starring Errol Flynn and Olivia De Havilland, which went on for several nights. The cinema was a hugely popular form of entertainment during those years and the two cinemas would be packed to capacity on Sunday nights as the townies were joined by their country cousins who cycled in from all points of the compass. Many of the clients who came in the Galway

Road and the Weir road would park their bicycles in the gardens of what they considered to be safe houses in Church View. They all had their own particular contacts and many a summer night, when they were at the pictures, we would have races up and down the street on bicycles that would have been left with us for safe keeping.

Reading comics was another serious occupation of our childhood and was a major source of engagement with like-minded enthusiasts. Swopping comics was a common pursuit of mine as only occasionally would I have the money to buy a brand new one, so that for the most part I depended on borrowed ones. My main sources were George Lyons and John Noel Ryan who always seemed to have a plentiful supply. The comics constituted a large part of our reading material and we followed the exploits of such characters as *Korky the Cat, Big Eggo* and *Desperate Dan* in the Dandy and the Beano from week to week with great enthusiasm. During the war those comics only came out on alternate weeks as paper was scarce and all the comics originated in England. George Lyons had a standing order for the weekly issues which appeared on Tuesdays. I often sat on the steps outside his house until he had finished reading his copy and sometimes succeeded in getting my hands on it before he had finished reading it himself. If one could accumulate a reasonable number of comics they became part of the currency of our boyhood economy. As we graduated to the more mature pages of the *Adventure*, the *Wizard* and the *Hotspur* we looked forward from week to week to reading the serialised adventures of our heroes particularly our sporting ones. Whilst Gaelic football and hurling were our favourite games we considered ourselves experts at soccer, rugby and cricket through our reading about those games in the comics even though we had never seen any live displays of them at the time.

The reading of comics was not encouraged by the Christian Brothers mainly, I believe, because of the fact that they emanated from England and were considered organs of propaganda at the time. The Brothers promoted their own magazine, *Our Boys*, which was started by the famous Brother Canice Craven who was a past pupil of Tuam CBS and who edited the magazine for many years. By contrast it contained only material with an Irish and nationalist flavour with tales of ancient manly heroes and stories associated with non-threatening characters like Kitty the Hare. It also had a page for jokes, and contributors to that section would be paid a half crown if they had their joke published. In his book, *Ancestral Voices*, Conor Cruise-O'Brien makes the claim that the same Brother Craven, who taught Padraig Pearse in Westland Row C.B.S., played a significant role in cultivating that patriot's political philosophy which culminated in the 1916 rebellion. A century later the current crop of historians are still debating the impact of that rebellion in the creation of the new state so I will leave the last words on that matter to those experts. However it might not be too far-fetched to say that we were all influenced by the 'ancestral voices' which hovered over the educational ethos of the Christian Brothers.

As well as comics, I was also an enthusiastic collector of stamps and other commodities such as pictures of footballers and hurlers which I would cut from the newspapers and paste into scrap-books or might exchange with other collector enthusiasts. On one occasion there was a series of national flags distributed in boxes of cigarettes which became collectors' items. They were quite colourful and came in an attractive silk-like material which fitted neatly between the pages of a book or copy. I had collected a few samples with a view to using them as collectors' currency and one day the Brother who was patrolling the classroom spotted one which caught his attention. Unfortunately for me it was a 'red rag to a bull' moment as the offending item was a Union Jack. 'I see we have a *Sasanach* in the class' he said loudly, drawing the attention of my classmates to the offending item. I hadn't taken into account the significance of such an item in the mind of the beholder whose favourite poem was *Sixteen Dead Men* by Dora Sigerson Shorter which he had been drilling into us all year and which had been written to commemorate the executed 1916 rebels. It had rousing passages such as

Sixteen dead men where do they go
To join their regiment where Sarsfield leads
Wolfe Tone and Emmet too, well do they know
There shall they bivouac telling great deeds.

I felt that I had committed a grave sin without fully appreciating why this colourful piece of cloth should evoke such a negative reaction and I wanted the ground to swallow me. To be called a *Sasanach* was

12. All around the Market House

In addition to its ecclesiastical status Tuam also had the reputation of being an important market town from the earliest years of the 20th century. Like many Irish towns and villages its principal economic role was in servicing its rural hinterland. On the Square the town's religious and economic aspects were represented by two focal points. One was the High Cross, the location of which was equidistant between the two cathedrals. This location was apparently an early compromise to satisfy competing claims of ownership. The second focal point was the Market House, a small building in the style of a Swiss chalet, which housed the apparatus for weighing potatoes and other farm produce and was operated by the local authority.

The area around the High Cross and the Market House was the nerve centre of Tuam, particularly on market and fair days when it throbbed with the rhythms of its rural supply lines. At other times it served the male population as a gathering point for discussing the topics of the day and as a useful vantage point from which to observe the passing parade. The High Cross and the Market House are no longer there, both having had to make way for the ever increasing demands of vehicular traffic; the former to a sheltered home in the local Church of Ireland cathedral and the latter to an unknown destination perhaps in some breaker's yard. The Market House was referred to, as follows, in a children's street rhyme which I heard from my late father:

'All around the Market House, All around the Market House,
All around the Market House and into Páidín Sweeney's.'

The hostelry referred to, to the best of my knowledge, became Browne's Pub in later years.

The principal market day was Saturday when the town became an open shop window displaying the abundant agricultural produce of the changing seasons. The Square was, paradoxically, more of a circle from which the main streets radiated to the four corners of the earth. It would fill up from early morning with horse and donkey-carts containing all kinds of agricultural produce. Regulars had traditional stands from where they would ply their wares. Potatoes were a staple diet for townsfolk and country-folk alike and a reputation for having 'good spuds' was an important asset for vendors who would develop long-standing relationships with satisfied customers mainly based on the quality of their produce.

The Saturday market was not confined to the Square and often spilled over to the adjoining streets and into the *Seamlas* at Vicar Street, particularly coming up to Christmas when cartloads of geese and turkeys would add to the volume of produce on sale. The *Seamlas* was also the place where turf was sold

The Square, Tuam

by the cartload. It was supplied mainly by men who came in the Weir Road from Woodquay and Sylane, travelling up Church View with their neatly built carts of turf with a bag of hay tied on top to feed the horse or donkey whilst they would be waiting to sell their wares. Sometimes they would have sold, before reaching the *Seamlas,* to customers along the route. This was also the venue for the sale of scollops (from the Irish word *scolb*), long sally rods which were used for securing the straw used for thatching.

Men cycled into town carrying braces of rabbits on the handlebars and carriers of their bicycles. The rabbits would have been snared during the week and they did a roaring trade on Saturday mornings particularly during the war years. There was even a market for the rabbit skins in those days. One supplier to my mother told me that if I sowed the legs of the graziers in the back garden I would have rabbits of my own to sell the following year.

Cabbage plants, in bundles of a hundred, and other vegetables were sold on the Square in front of Butler's drapery shop, and visiting dealers from farther afield had stalls on the Square near the Town Hall where they sold delph and all sorts of haberdashery. Their marketing patter provided amusement for onlookers and customers alike. There was an open-air butcher's stall on the Square from which meat was sold without any danger of interference from health authorities or EU regulations.

At the corner of the Town Hall, poultry of every description was sold on Saturdays by Mrs Trayers, ably assisted by Paddy McKenna, and fresh herrings from the Dublin Fish Market were sold there on Fridays by Mike and Mrs Ralph. Later on his son, Big Miko, took over that stand and, in addition to fish, sold vegetables when in season. I recall an occasion when I was asked by one of the Brothers to run an errand for Celia Byrne, their housekeeper, who had apparently run short of vegetables for the dinner which she was preparing in the monastery kitchen on that particular day. I was so glad to get out of the classroom that I hit off down town, and had reached the Square, before I realised that I had overlooked asking Celia which shop I was to go to for the vegetables. Not wishing to return to the school empty handed, I approached Big Miko and explained my predicament. He generously offered me two heads of cabbage and I returned to school with my hands full. I am not sure if Celia had intended to have cabbage on the menu that day but I didn't hang around to find out and didn't hear any more about it. I was never requisitioned thereafter to carry out such an important task. I don't know if Miko Ralph ever got paid but whenever I think of that occasion I am always reminded that one of my father's favourite sayings was that 'two heads are better than one even if they are only heads of cabbage'.

Suckling calves and bonivs (from the Irish word *banbh*), were sold from the backs of carts on High Street, near the old graveyard, and they were also sold on the Square near the Town Hall from an improvised corral manned by Luke Smyth and his trusty assistant, Gus Jordan, who wore a soft hat in the cowboy style. Prospective customers gathered round bargaining and tangling over the fare on offer. For juvenile townie onlookers the buzz was exciting. On one such occasion, Gus was being badgered by a rural gentleman for a substantial discount on one of the specimens on sale. Amongst the consignment on offer there was one which apparently had certain deficiencies as far as its breeding potential was concerned. After an extended bargaining session, Gus approached his senior colleague for directions and addressed him as follows in the local vernacular:

'Sight the buff sham in the back hammer.

He's lookin' for a choicer.

Will I slip him the chat with the gammy hoppers?'

Having got the necessary nod of approval, Gus returned to complete the transaction and sent another satisfied customer away with a doubtful bargain. Being something of an innocent abroad at the time I didn't then fully comprehend the anatomy underlying that commercial exchange and it was only after extensive further education in the basic facts of life that the penny finally dropped. The moral of that story has to be *caveat emptor!*

Fair days were busy occasions when the town was all activity. When we were going to school the October fairs in Tuam were amongst the largest fairs in the west of Ireland. The big sheep fair was held on Tuesday and the big cattle fair was held on the Wednesday. On those days the streets would be jammed with cattle and sheep all the way from the Fairgreen on Tullinadaly Road, up through Shop Street and the Square and down Vicar Street to the Railway Station. If there was some gridlock along Vicar Street, whilst waiting for an extra supply of empty wagons at the station cattle bank, one might be recruited to help mind the livestock whilst the owner dropped into the Rustic Vaults for some refreshments. There would be smaller fairs of horses and pigs during that week and the schools would close. It was our equivalent of the modern mid-term break. Many towns hosted such fairs before the marts took over. The fairs were great social events as well and people would avail of the opportunity to meet and greet neighbours and friends and to carry out business transactions of one kind or another. And the Square was the focal point where town and country mingled.

The Square was also the principal venue for all outdoor public meetings. In the forties, election campaigns were a great spectator sport. After-mass and fair-day meetings were the normal means by which aspiring candidates got their messages across to the electorate from an improvised platform or the back of a lorry and without the benefit of amplification of any kind. The big pre-election rallies would be held on a Saturday evening or on a Sunday morning after last mass when

Crowd at election meeting on square- mid 1940s

large crowds would gather in the Square to hear the speeches from the platform in front of the Town Hall. Strong voices and hard necks were essential qualifications for success at the hustings and heckling was a regular occurrence when candidates would be left in no doubt as to the validity of their credentials.

I remember one occasion in the mid 1940's when the then Taoiseach, Eamon de Valera, came to Tuam to address an election rally. Some of us youngsters went out the Tullinadaly Road to join in the excitement of his impending visit. He was escorted into town by a torchlight procession of his party's faithful who carried paraffin-soaked sods of turf held aloft on hay forks. As the car bearing Mr de Valera came by, the driver stopped at a point down near the Demesne where our group was waiting to view the passing parade and, lowering the car window, *An Taoiseach* greeted us in Irish. We ventured some replies in the native tongue and were eventually relieved by Mrs Gormally who arrived on the scene and took over the conversation. She was a good Irish speaker who had more than the *cúpla focal* to exchange with him. Later on that evening, from the back of a lorry on the Square, he opened his address to the populace of Tuam by expressing his delight at the fact that a group of children were able to converse with him in the native tongue as he entered our historic town. This, he declared, augured well for the future of the native language which had a high priority in his government's plans for the wellbeing of the country. Mr de Valera dominated the political scene for 15 of the 18 years that I spent in Tuam and among the local personalities who kept the political pot boiling in those days were Mark Kilillea, Mick Donnellan and Bobby Burke each of whom were lustily supported by their own disciples and attracted their own share of loyal followers. Election campaigns nowadays do not hold the same attraction as they did when I first became aware of what they were all about. Today they are driven in the main by the media who determine the form they will take from beginning to end. By publishing pre-election polls and providing photo opportunities for the candidates and reporting the most colourful sound bites the media very subtly dictates the style of each campaign. The real 'jizz' as far as the local supporters are concerned has gone out of what used to be exciting occasions.

The High Cross, Tuam
Source: National Library of Ireland

13. Good Scouting

Sometime in the early forties I joined the boy scouts, or to be more precise the 2nd Galway Troop of the Catholic Boy Scouts of Ireland. There was a good tradition of scouting in Tuam and there was also a troop of Girl Guides but in those days never the twain did meet, at least not formally. Meetings were held every week in the Scout Hall on the Old Road next to the LDF hall. There we learned the rules of scouting as we prepared for the serious business of being invested as Rawley scouts. The rules were religious and patriotic in tone emphasising that, after loyalty to God and country, the duty of the scout began in the home. At that point in our young lives the prospect of adventures in the great outdoors was much more important and immediate than the religious and political aspirations of the parent organisation. Nevertheless we considered ourselves ready for all eventualities by adhering to the scout motto *Bí Ullamh*! (Be Prepared). We did our drills and wore our uniforms with pride and new words like neckerchief, lanyard and woggle entered our vocabulary. We practiced the three-fingered salute and the left-handed handshake and gained merit badges for being able to perform various kinds of tests. We played games like 'cock-fighting' and 'Murphy says' and learned how to tie knots with fancy names such as the 'sheepshank', the 'bow line' and the 'carrick bend'. The fact that I never found occasion to use any of those rope techniques in later life is irrelevant. We also learned the semaphore method of flag signalling using two flags to spell out warning messages to distant lookouts who were expected to be able to relay the message accurately to the next lookout post. It was a rather ponderous method of communication which, thankfully, we didn't have to resort to in real life. With the advent of the mobile phone I presume it has become redundant.

One of our main activities was hiking to Gardenfield wood on Sundays. We spent many happy summer days in that peaceful setting on the banks of the river Clare. Presumably we had permission from the owners to use that fantastic natural amenity which, like many other features of old Tuam,

Scout Hiking in the paddock in Gardenfield

is no longer available. In the middle of the wood there was a green space called 'The Paddock' where we played football and rounders and became experts at pitching tents, and lighting fires made with sticks and fallen branches of trees gathered in the adjoining woodland. There we boiled water and made copious amounts of smoke flavoured Irish stew with ingredients brought from home. At autumn time, among the fallen woodland leaves, we gathered acorns to use as ammunition in mock battles and collected chestnuts for playing conkers.

Another of our hiking venues was Ballinderry Castle, out the Athenry Road, and on occasions we went out to Lewin's Castle in Castlegrove for our Sunday hike. Hiking is something of a misnomer as most of the time we cycled to those venues. On one occasion we went as far as Moylough where we set up stall in the lawn in front of the parochial house and, having eaten, spent the afternoon exploring the

Scout Hike to Ballinderry Castle late 1940's

Includes from left: Brian Waldron, John Waldron, Tom Leo (partly hidden), Brendan McEnnis, Jackie O'Sullivan, Morgan O'Connell, AN Other, Michael Cooley, Paddy Kilgarriff (partly hidden), Peter Cooley, Gabriel Maloney and Tommy Kelly.

hidden mysteries of that village. As it was considered too far for me to cycle, the scoutmaster at the time, Jarlath Noone, gave me a lift on the bar of his bicycle all the way there and back, a total of about 25 miles.

I remember Sunday excursions to Silver Strand in the back of Jim Moggan's lorry. At that time you could drive right onto the sand and on one occasion when it was time to go home in the evening the wheels wouldn't grip on the sand and we had to go into the nearby wood to break branches of trees to put under the tyres. Then all got behind the lorry and pushed until it took off. There were summer camps to Barna and Spiddal where we swam all day and fished for mackerel which came in shoals to the piers near where we were camped. Eamon Holian and Paddy Tierney from Ballygaddy Rd. operated as cooks for the duration of the two-week camps. At night time we sat around the campfire singing the summer nights away. A special treat on those camping holidays was

Tuam Boy Scout Troop: Outside Scout Hall 1948
Back Row: Tom Leo, Eamon Lynch, Sean Higgins, Miko Walshe, Paddy Egan, John Staunton, Tommy Kelly, Paschal O'Brien, Jarlath Burke. Front Row: Brendan Mc Ennis, Tommy Murphy, Morgan O'Connell, Brian Waldron, Miko Kelly, Fabian Walshe, Brendan O'Connell, Kilian Walshe, P.J Grealish.

to cycle into Galway with my Eagle patrol companions for tea and buns in Lydon's café in Shop St There were occasional visits to Ballyhaunis where we joined up with the local troop and on another occasion a scout jamboree in Listowel which was attended by scouts from all over Ireland.

At Christmas time we had an annual 'feast' by courtesy of a ladies committee made up mainly of some mothers who put on a big spread for us in the Scout Hall with lashings of buns and sweet cake and lemonade. I remember, having gorged ourselves almost to the point of sickness, carrying out supplies stuffed inside my scout tunic to some school pals who were not in the scouts but who, by prior arrangement, would be waiting across the Old Road at the back gate into Comerford's house where the booty was transferred to willing hands. We would then return to continue with the festivities in the Scout Hall.

Scout Group c1950/51
Front Row: Liam O'Connell, Pat Waldron, Tommy Kelly, George Staunton, Miko Donnellan, Brian Waldron, Paul Seavers. 2nd Row: Conal O'Connell, Donal Kennedy, Frankie Quinn, Paul O'Connell, Liam Gallagher, Sean Greaney Tommy Murphy. 3rd Row: Murt McCormack, Frank Staunton, Midie Loftus, Diarmuid Maloney, Mickey Seavers, Philip Joyce, Pat Leo, Pat Griffith. Back Row: Patrick Moran, Jarlath Burke, John Kennedy, Noel Loftus, Billy Lynch, Eamon Lynh, Gabriel Maloney.

And we had the pipe band, membership of which was open to all willing to give it a try. There were three stages in the initiation process for would-be pipers. In the first instance you were given a chanter to learn the fingering. This was done under the tutelage of a senior member of the band who had gone through the same process at an earlier stage and who taught one how to play the various tunes which made up the band's repertoire. If one survived this stage, potential pipers were allocated a set of bagpipes on which they learned how to keep the bag filled and the chanter playing. Keeping the bag filled required considerable wind power. The last stage was to master the art of blowing, fingering and marching at the same time and in unison with the other members of the band. Easier said than done and some of the more delicate souls fell by the wayside en route.

After a session in the Scout Hall one Saturday morning, being an enthusiastic beginner, I was allowed to bring the pipes home to do some further practice. My neighbour across the street was granted a similar concession. When I arrived home I went into the bedroom, it being the only free space available to me at the time, and launched into a recital. The resulting din alerted my mother who came rushing into the room, presumably to see if somebody was being strangled. When she discovered the source of the din she was not impressed and I was ordered out of the house, as mothers of large families had enough problems without having to tolerate a bag-piper in one of the bedrooms. The only venue available in the circumstances was the old reliable *Culán*. Tommy Murphy had met with a similar reception and, in what might be described as an act of mutual solidarity, we completed our first serious public recital there in the open air with an audience of children from the street who, on hearing strange sounds, had followed the Pied pipers of Church View to a scene which was never to be repeated.

The band consisted of approximately half a dozen pipers, two or three kettle drummers and one on the big drum. On special occasions we were supplemented by two or three flag-bearers. At times when a full complement of real pipers was not available 'dummy' pipers were conscripted to stand in for the absentees. They were tutored to maintain appearances and to act as if they were really blowing. To offset possible discordant contributions on the part of the replacements, the drones and reeds would be removed from their instruments so that we had the phenomenon of silent bagpipes. I must emphasise that this practice was only resorted to in dire emergency situations, was strictly confidential and known only to insiders. However on a number of occasions while on my way to the scout hall I was accosted by two 'gentlemen' from Tullinadaly Road who frequented the area around the Odeon Cinema and Ryan's Cafe. They obviously had heard rumours and would demand to know if

Tuam Boy Scouts Pipe Band c1950
Back Row: P.J.Grealish, Tommy Murphy, Tommy Kelly, Miko Donnellan, Liam O'Connell, Kevin O'Brien, Eamonn Lynch. Front Row: George Staunton, Brian Waldron, Conall O'Connell.

it was true that some of the pipers were not the real thing and that they were only 'gammin on' to be playing. I would never admit to our dark secret, always insisted that I was the genuine article and that if there were silent pipers I certainly was not one of them. They were sceptical to say the least. Thereafter, to avoid running the gauntlet of Shop St., I would take a short cut down the Mall and then down the Herring Lane, as it was called by the older people, on my way to the Scout Hall when the band was scheduled for parade. This lack of appreciation of our efforts was reflected in the attitude of some rival musicians as, I believe, that Danny Kelly who was the master of the local Brass Band used to refer to us as the windbags and threaten malingers in his outfit with deportation to our ranks if they didn't measure up to his standards.

The band led the troop on parades to the various events around the town which the scouts attended. It also played at football matches and annually ushered in the New Year with a recital on the Square at midnight on New Year's Eve. In 1947 we met the St Jarlath's team on its arrival at the outskirts of the town on the Monday after they had won the All Ireland Colleges competition for the first time and led the parade to the Square where a bonfire blazed and they were given a great welcome by the townspeople. I think the band added a colourful dimension to such occasions and to the various public events which we supported and, dare I say it, even to the musical life of Tuam during those years. At that time *Fáinne Geal an Lae* was the main plank in our modest repertoire and regardless of which version of that ancient tune I hear from time to time it never fails to ring a nostalgic bell.

On one occasion we played at a dance in Cortoon hall, being billed as a special attraction. I remember that occasion for another reason. Our 'recital' took place during an interval in the dance and when we had finished we watched with great interest from the sidelines as the dancers took to the floor. It was the first time I had ever been at a real dance and, having at this stage abandoned our bagpipes, I had the temerity to ask a young lady to dance even though I had never attempted that activity before. Freda Murphy, my neighbour from Church View, was kind enough to guide me on my first trip into the light fantastic via an Old Time waltz and thereby opened up new vistas beyond the world of pipe bands and scouting.

My last outing with the scouts before leaving Tuam in 1952 was in a concert in the Odeon Cinema organised by the scouts in aid of local charities. We opened the concert with campfire songs. The guest artist on that occasion was Dermot Troy, a fine tenor who died at a young age. Winifred O'Dea, a well-known and popular singer at that time, also took part in that concert and the accompanist was Maureen Dillon who was a native of the town. I still have the programme from that particular occasion with Dermot Troy's autograph and his message wishing me *'Good Scouting'*.

I have good memories of those years in the scouts and of the friendships made, some of which lasted over time and distance. In particular I remember Sean Higgins and Billy Lynch who always remained in touch with a fellow 'exile'. Alas they, like too many of our scouting companions, have already departed for the *Campfire in the Sky* but their memory remains ever fresh and will always evoke the vibrancy of boyhood. Scouting played an important role in our young lives and great credit is due to those who provided leadership in the organisation over the years. During most of my time in the scouts in Tuam, P.J. Grealish was the scoutmaster and he was exemplary in that role. I'm glad to see that he is still hale and hearty as I write these recollections and would like, on my own behalf at least, to belatedly acknowledge his contribution to an important phase of our youthful world.

PART I.

Tuam Boy Scouts . . . . . Campfire Songs

Brendan O'Gorman . . . . Comedian

WINIFRED O'DEA (Soprano)

" In Those Soft Silken Curtains " (Puccini)

" Scenes That Are Brightest "

" My Hero."

MAUREEN DILLON, A.L.C.M. (Piano)

" Legend of the Glass Mountain."

DERMOT TROY (Tenor)

" Serenade " from " The Fair Maid of Perth " (Bizet)

" Because " (Guy d'Hardelot)

" At the Mid Hour of Night " (Thomas Moore).

CONCERTED ITEM

Dermot Troy   -   Winifred O'Dea

Duet from Act I, " La Boheme."

PART II.

Brendan O'Gorman . . . . Comedian

WINIFRED O'DEA (Soprano)

" Invitation to the Dance " (Weber)

" Love and Music " (Puccini).

MAUREEN DILLON (Piano)

Hungarian Rhapsody No. 2 (Liszt).

DERMOT TROY (Tenor)

" None Shall Sleep To-night " (Puccini)

" Down Her Pale Cheek " (Donizetti).

ACCOMPANIST . . . . MAUREEN DILLON, A.L.C.M.

Odeon Cinema, Tuam,

Friday Night, May 30th, 1952.

Curtain: 8.30 p.m.

GRAND
CELEBRITY CONCERT

DERMOT TROY

(" THE IRISH CARUSO ")

and

WINIFRED O'DEA

(Celebrated Cork Soprano).

PRESENTED BY TUAM CATHOLIC BOY SCOUTS
IN AID OF LOCAL CHARITIES.

Souvenir Programme.

TUAM HERALD, TUAM.

Celebrity Concert Programme - 1952

118

Galway Team 1948

Back Row L to R: Charlie Connolly (with hat), Tom Sullivan, Ned Keogh, Johnny Dunne, T.J.Mooney, Tom Connern, Joe Duggan, Jackie Mangan, Paddy Ryan, Kieran Hunt. Front Row L to R: Frank Stockwell, Frank Quinn, Pat McManus, John Glynn, Brendan Hanniffy, Seamus O'Rourke, Sean Thornton, Jarlath Canavan, Sean Purcell.

of the match, the contraband was successfully smuggled in, wrapped in a soutane and surplice in a mass-servers duffel bag. During the summer and Easter holidays, the townies made great use of the college field and the ball alley when the boarders would be on vacation.

Most of us can recall a summer from childhood against which all other summers are found wanting. Patrick Kavanagh describes such a summer in eloquently simple language as

    ' -------- the Warm Summer, that landmark

    In a child's mind, an infinite day --

    The whole summer during the school holidays

    Till the blackberries appeared.

    Yes, a tremendous time that summer stands

    Beyond the grey finities of normal weather.'

For this writer, 1948 was such a summer. It was not because of the weather but because that particular summer the Galway football team spent six eventful weeks in full-time training in Tuam in preparation for the Connacht Final and replay. For that brief period, Tuam became, the centre of the football universe for those of us who were interested in football. After a lean period since 1945 the county team reached the Connacht Final. That was the team above any other which, as far as I am concerned, refutes the old sporting cliché that losers are quickly forgotten for it was that team which started many of my generation on the path of affliction which, as followers of the Galway team, we have trodden for over half a century.

Most of the team members who were not from the town stayed in the Odeon Cafe in Shop Street which at that time was run by Kevin and Mrs Doyle. Every morning they would start training in the Fairgreen under the direction of John 'Tull' Dunne from Ballinasloe who was the County Secretary as well as the trainer of the team at that time. They would tog out in the LDF hall and the morning session was spent running around the adjoining Fairgreen. Toddy Ryan from Ballymote was always on hand to give the magic rub to the more seasoned players and the smell of wintergreen filled the air.

As loyal camp followers Hauleen McDonagh and I had the job of providing 'state-of-the art' showering facilities for the players. These consisted of a tin bath filled with water from a nearby pump. Tull had a hose attached which he used to hose down the players after their morning session ended, with one of his assistants on a hand-pump. The water was cold and he would put in Gentian Violet crystals, presumably to ensure compliance with whatever hygiene regulations were considered appropriate at the time. Jimmy Moran had a pick-up truck and acted as chauffeur to Tull and the less energetic team members, driving them to the afternoon sessions of football in Parkmore and in the evenings to play clock-golf in the tennis court out the Ballymote Road. There would always be room in the back of the pick-up truck for the regular hangers-on. I remember some members of the team were taken on a tour of the Beet Factory on one occasion and were shown around by Jimmy Keating and Matty Murphy. It was the only time I ever saw the inside of the Beet Factory as we followed them everywhere and were always tolerated. On some afternoons the players relaxed playing cards on the banks of the river in Gardenfield. There was no sponsorship or foreign holidays going in those days and I guess that expenses for players or officials, if there were any, didn't amount to much. As the day of the Connacht Final approached the excitement mounted and the big question was if we would be able to go to Roscommon for the match. In the event a large contingent left on the excursion train from Tuam and there was a certain sense of anti-climax when the match ended in a draw as we all felt of course that Galway should have won. The compensation was that there was another period of full-time training in Tuam where our services as water carriers were again required. Defeat by Mayo in the replay left us demoralised. That Mayo team went on to win 2 All-Irelands and Galway went into decline for a few years but the stalwarts of 1948 have not been forgotten.

At that time there was great talk of the need for a new stadium in Tuam and a committee of townspeople and GAA people was set up for that purpose. The venue earmarked for development was Campbell's field in Vicarschorland which had been purchased by the Tuam Stars club in 1946. It was just around the corner from Church View near the Railway Station and I remember a few unofficial football matches being played there before the development really started after it was taken over by the Tuam Stadium Development Association in 1948.

Johnny Griffey who became the foreman on the site when the development started used to exercise his greyhounds there occasionally.

Around that time the word went around that a well-known local character, Martin Tighe (affectionately known as 'Bully'), had invented an 'electric hare', with the intention of eventually being in a position to compete with the Greyhound Track in Galway. One day, at the urging of some of his 'friends', he decided to try out his new invention in what could be termed a 'real-time' experiment in Campbell's field with one of Johnny Griffey's greyhounds. He arrived at the field with an elaborate contraption piled high on his bicycle. When laid out it consisted of a second bicycle and a large quantity of old bicycle chains linked together to form a sort of conveyor belt. When in place the finished product consisted of the two upturned bicycles, placed at what then seemed to be a respectable distance apart, which were linked together by the long length of bicycle chains. The theory of operation was to manually turn the pedals of one of the bikes to get the 'conveyor belt' moving and gradually build up speed. When the whole apparatus was in place the final piece of the jig-saw was added. It consisted of a rabbit skin which was tied to the 'assembly-line' to act as a lure for any interested greyhound. It was 'Bully's' intention to do a couple of practice runs to test the operational capacity of his invention before subjecting it to a live run but, before his fragile prototype had gathered any momentum on its maiden run, Johnny slipped the greyhound which was literally champing at the bit and before anyone could shout 'stop' it had grabbed the rabbit skin and taken off across Campbell's field with the whole contraption disintegrating and scattering in its wake. Another great idea had failed to achieve its imaginative objective and as the main protagonists gathered up their respective properties and departed the scene, both in high dudgeon, there were some colourful comments exchanged between them as to their respective competencies.

The development of the new stadium was a notable event in our lives. It was the first time that we were introduced to the concept of voluntary labour as this became an important input into the construction of the new pitch. The boundary walls were built by contract and several local men were employed full time in the construction of the concrete seating and perimeter walls under the direction of Harry Finnegan, a young local engineer, and supervised by the afore-mentioned Johnny Griffey and Jim Geraghty. As enthusiastic supporters of the project we readily became part of an army of voluntary labourers of every class and occupation. The original clay had to be removed from the field because it was found to be non-porous. Then a system of French drains was constructed and the whole area was covered by a layer of cinders

Workmen on the new stadium c1950

Front Row: John O'Grady, Paddy Collins, Tom Larkin, Johnny Griffey, Bill Naughton. Back Row: AN Other, AN Other, Mattie Kelly, Tony Nicholson, John Mannion

more than two feet in depth before layers of new clay were added. This voluntary activity reached its peak in the spring of 1949 as young and old, boys and men ranging from schoolboys to senior citizens, spent all the daylight hours working shoulder to shoulder to ensure that the new grass seed would be in on time for the new pitch to have a carpet of green on the planned opening day in the following summer. And nobody worried about health and safety or insurance issues in those days.

Many lorries, including CIE ones, were employed to haul cinders from the Beet Factory during the development work. One day, being a regular and willing volunteer, I had parked my bike against a pile of cinders and Bosco McCabe, with possibly more important things on his mind, reversed his lorry over it leaving me with a warped wheel. When I brought it to his attention, with a certain amount of trepidation, he told me to go down to Moran's garage and tell Joe Davin to fix the wheel and to send the bill to Mr. McCabe. Both Bosco and Joe were well-known residents of Church View. Joe asked me who Mr McCabe

Tuam Stadium Development Committee, 1950

Front: Tommy Hannon, Brother Wrafter, Hugh Mangan, Joe Heskin, Michael Cahill, Jimmy Moran, John Joe Egan. 2nd Row: Paddy Farrell, P.J.Mills, Ned Farrell, Harry Finnegan, Jim Geraghty, Steven Long, Jack Mooney. 3rd Row: Paddy Prendergast, Miko Kelly, John O'Reilly, Luke O'Brien, Benny Connaughton, Tom McHugh, Patty O'Connor. 4th Row: Dan McCormack, Michael Connaughton, Joe Mooney, Jarlath O'Connell, Jack Cughlan. At Back: Johnny Griffey and Brendan Burke. Inset: Fr. Mooney and D.P. Kennedy.

Because of the scarcity of foreign items the importance of the farming contribution was continually stressed. If the weather was bad at harvesting times it added to the problem of supply. It was common to have prayers said at mass for a good harvest which highlighted the problems and brought them to the attention of townspeople. The state of emergency generated by the war continued for some time afterwards and in 1946 the weather at harvest time was so bad that the harvesting was seriously delayed and youths and men from the town were rounded up to go out and help local farmers to save the crops. One Sunday there was an announcement in the cathedral that lorries would be available in the square after mass to transport volunteers out to the local farms to help with the harvesting. George Lyons and I went up to the Square to offer our assistance in this national effort but we were rejected as being unsuitable for the tasks involved. Nothing daunted, we went home and collected our bicycles and cycled out the Galway Road. A couple of miles out the road, beyond Cloonfush, we saw an elderly couple working in a field binding oats. We dismounted, climbed over the fence and asked them if they needed help. Neither of us had much of a clue as to what was required but the man showed us how to make 'stooks' of the oats and we got the hang of it after a while and worked away all the evening with the couple and by the time we were finished the field of oats was standing. I think they were amused at first but thanked us profusely when we were leaving. I can still remember that day vividly with a great sense of satisfaction at a job well done.

That particularly wet autumn and winter was followed by an extended spell of cold weather through February and March, 1947, with heavy snowfalls which covered the ground for weeks. The *Tuam Herald* reported that on Monday night, 24th February, Tuam had its heaviest snowfall of the month-old cold spell.

'All through Monday night and Tuesday there was a driving snow storm - the worst for many years – and roads were covered to a depth of about six inches. Then on Tuesday afternoon a thaw set in which raised hopes of an end to the Arctic weather. Light rain and sleet followed and by night the streets were inches deep in slush. --- -- Greatest surprise still was to come – Tuesday night's thaw turned to frost and on Wednesday the slushy roads were crusted with ice and frozen snow. Snow fell in flurries on Wednesday and brilliant sunshine followed for short intervals.'

I have reason to remember that occasion well because my Uncle Berney, who was also my godfather, died suddenly at his work in the Post Office on the Monday of that week and his funeral was held on the Wednesday. He had been a member of the Old IRA and the report of his death in the *Tuam Herald* stated that a guard of honour of Old IRA men marched behind the hearse and his coffin, draped with the Tricolour, was carried to the graveside by his colleagues in Tuam Post Office. I can still clearly recall the sound of their marching footsteps crunching through the frozen snow as we followed the cortege to his graveside in the New Cemetery.

16. Big Issues

For most Irish families since the time of the famine, emigration to America and Britain especially, has been a constant feature. Its scale and pattern would have varied from generation to generation but the exodus has continued to impact significantly on those destinations right up to the present time. Some years ago, while in New York, I visited Ellis Island which was the main entry point into the USA for immigrants up until the 1950's. There is a museum there which contains memorabilia from all over Europe. These were donated by the descendants of the people who went to the New World in droves in the late 19th and early 20th century in search of a better life. There were all sorts of items, particularly from the eastern European countries, which reflected the cultures and life-styles of their owners. Gold and silver jewellery, timber and bone carvings, fine-cut glassware and various items of clothing containing intricate lace work and embroidery predominated and there were many books including leather-bound bibles in the languages of the immigrants.

I was surprised to find that there was very little in the museum of Irish origin. Knowing that thousands of Irish immigrants had arrived through Ellis Island I was curious to find out what kind of material had found its way with them across the Atlantic. I could identify only three such items in the whole museum, a blackthorn stick, a donkey shoe and a set of rosary beads. I imagined some young man leaving his rural home and taking the humble stick as a reminder of where he came from. The donkey shoe may have been packed into a travelling bag with the hope that it would bring the traveller good luck. A horseshoe might have been too heavy or maybe they didn't own a horse. The rosary beads represented what the majority of them valued most and made up for their lack of earthly valuables.

This experience brought home to me the fact that the pattern of Irish emigration during that period was different to that of people from the European mainland. The latter tended to emigrate in large groups, often entire families leaving and bringing all their belongings with no intention of returning. The Irish tended to emigrate as individuals, in the main young single men and women, who left with not much more than the clothes on their backs, their personal belongings in a cardboard suitcase and with the address of a relative or neighbour who would put them up until they were able to fend for themselves in their new surroundings. It also reminded me of an incident which my mother recounted many years ago.

In our sitting room she had a china cabinet in which she kept all her best china, delph and other bits and pieces. One day I was searching for something and found a single cup with a picture of her local home town in Co. Mayo. I assumed it was the last survivor of an ancient set and asked her about it. It had its own story. When she was a young girl in the early years of the 20th century most of the young people from her area emigrated as soon as they could. Usually a number of people from the same village or townland would travel together and there would be what was called an 'American Wake' before they left when the neighbours would all gather to wish them *bon voyage*. On one such occasion her two older sisters were among those emigrating and they had been preparing for some weeks for the journey. They had visited the local town to purchase various items including those needed for the long journey by boat from Queenstown to America. At that time passengers had to fend for themselves in the course of the voyage. This necessitated providing utensils for the preparation and consumption of food and drink. The cup was one of the items which her sister had acquired for the journey.

On the night before her departure one of the neighbours, who had been in the United States and who was something of a 'hob lawyer', was advising the departing ones about the hazards of the journey and told them that they would have to throw all the utensils, which they used on the journey, overboard before their arrival as they wouldn't be allowed to take them ashore. When her sister heard this she decided that she wouldn't bring the cup as it would break her heart to have to throw the cup with the picture of her home town into the ocean. So, instead of the cup, she put a tin mug from the dresser in the kitchen into her luggage and gave the cup to her little sister as a keepsake. I don't know what happened to the cup but I suspect it was given to a member of the next generation who eventually brought it across the Atlantic as a memento of its original owner who never made it back to this side.

Moving forward to our generation, the subject of emigration was seriously exercising the minds of the local hierarchy during the nineteen thirties and forties, in particular its spiritual implications. In Tuam in 1938 the co-adjutor to the elderly Archbishop Gilmartin, was Most Rev Dr Walsh who had the title of Bishop of Cela. In April of that year he visited Cortoon where he addressed the congregation on the occasion of the blessing of a new bell which had been donated to the local church. He offered the following advice on the problem of emigration, as reported in the following week's edition of the *Tuam Herald*:

'There is no man so really prosperous as the man who has his own farm, his own homestead. He may not have a lot of money to spend but he can lead a healthy happy life at home and he is never in danger of starvation. I want to impress on all of you that the rush from the countryside to the cities and towns is a capital mistake, a national calamity. Many of those who took part in the rush are now very threatened, very much disillusioned: instead of amassing wealth, as they had expected, they find it very hard to make ends meet: it is no exaggeration to say that some are actually on the brink of starvation.

Whatever may be said about changing to one of our Irish towns or cities, no boy or girl ought to emigrate to England without giving the question most serious consideration. I have no hesitation in saying that unrestricted emigration to England constitutes a grave danger to the faith; while on the other side the emigrant, so far from amassing a fortune, may have to face unemployment and all its consequences.

The real wealth of a country is in the land: and the backbone of this country, like every other country is the tiller of the soil. The man who works the land must command our respect and admiration. I hope our legislators and all classes of the community will realise this and take to heart what one of our poets said long ago:-

'A bold peasantry, their country's pride,
When once destroyed, can never be supplied'.

The following month the annual Tuam Feis was held over the course of three days and consisted of drama, language, music and dancing competitions in which all the schools in the town and surrounding areas participated. It was officially opened on Sunday 15th May in the Mall Cinema by Archbishop Gilmartin. In the course of his address at the Feis he continued the theme of his co-adjutor, referring to emigration as being the **second great evil** affecting the country at that time. Accepting that there must be emigration 'more or less' he stated:

'--- I think it a pity to see our youth, who could do well enough at home, leaving the green fields and genial atmosphere of rural Ireland, attracted more by the garish amusements of the cities than by the certainty of finding in them suitable employment.

18. Epilogue

I left Tuam on the early train on a fine July morning in 1952 one month after doing the Leaving Cert. in the local C.B.S. By coincidence three other young men from outside Tuam, who had also attended the C.B.S., were travelling on the train that morning. I was going to Dublin to take up a clerical position with Córas Iompair Eireann and they were going to England. To paraphrase John B Keane, 'many young men (and women) of twenty (and younger) were saying goodbye' at railway stations all over Ireland at that time in the latest wave of emigration which was seen by many of my contemporaries as part of the natural order of things. It was not surprising therefore that, in the course of the journey to Dublin, the merits of going to England, even if only for the summer, were discussed and I began to get the feeling that my companions on the journey had chosen the better option. When the train arrived at Westland Row station we walked along Pearse Street as far as O'Connell Bridge. I had an appointment to be at Kingsbridge station at 1 p.m. for an interview and medical examination and the others were travelling by the mail-boat to Holyhead that evening. We arranged to meet again under the clock outside Clerys on O'Connell St at 6 o'clock. I intended to accompany them to Westland Row to 'see them off' on the train to Dun Laoghaire from where they would catch the mail boat to Holyhead.

When I arrived at Kingsbridge I was instructed by a man in the Personnel Office to go to the office of the Chief Medical Officer for an examination and to return afterwards to him for further instructions.

CIE Engine and Passenger Train – Tuam Station 1952
Source: 'A Decade of Steam', Railway Preservation Society of Ireland 1974.

I did as directed and duly returned to the first port of call. After some time I was called into an inner office and informed, quite casually, that I had failed the eyesight test and therefore was not eligible to take up the position which I had been offered. It was the first time I had ever had an eyesight test and it was news to me that I had a problem. I can't remember being unduly worried and left Kingsbridge without further ado believing that was the end of the matter. I am still bemused at how easily I departed the scene without asking any questions.

My sister, Josephine, lived in Dublin at the time and I had arranged to meet her somewhere near the city centre that afternoon. When we met up she asked me how I had got on and I told her that I hadn't got the job. She questioned me further as to the reason and asked me what I was going to do now. I said 'I think I'll go to England with the lads', explaining about my travelling companions of the morning. 'You will do no such thing,' she said and insisted that I was either to go home on the evening train or I could stay with her for a few days until I got things cleared up. I agreed, somewhat reluctantly, to the latter arrangement but said I would follow her home later as I had promised to meet up with my companions of the morning at Clerys at 6 o'clock. I met them as we had arranged, accompanied them back to Westland Row and waited with them until the train left for Dun Laoghaire. Afterwards, with certain misgivings, I walked back alone along Pearse Street to catch a bus to my sister's house. I have never met any of those lads since. Some of them may have returned to Ireland later on but the one I knew best, who was a classmate of mine, didn't come back. As far as I know he emigrated to Canada at a later date.

On the following day my brother-in-law rang the Personnel Office in Kingsbridge to check out the facts. He was told that if I got glasses I could come back in and I would be given the job. I started my working career the following Friday in the Booking Office at Harcourt Street station, equipped with a brand new pair of spectacles. From then on I began to see the world in a whole new light in more ways than one. I spent the next three months of that summer in Dublin during which time one of the highlights for me was the thrill of watching the Galway minor team winning their first All-Ireland football title with fellow townies and contemporaries, Brian Waldron and Tommy Brosnan, on the team and enjoying the victory celebrations in the Mansion House that night.

I have often wondered what might have been had I taken the Holyhead boat on that day in 1952. The fact that I thought of going to England with my travelling companions, however ill-prepared, were it not for sisterly intervention, indicates that fate plays a big role in much of our destinies. For many who did go, there may have been no turning back but there were others who kept in touch with the place which formed them, even if only in spirit. In my own case the distance I travelled was short and would not be classed as emigration, but one has only to examine the family tree to realise that for most Irish families, particularly large ones, emigration has been a common feature in every generation.

The northern writer, Benedict Kiely, has described the first 18 years of a person's life as the most impressionable and formative years, the ones that 'fix you for what you are'. I spent those years in Tuam and, insofar as I am now writing about them over 60 years later, I can't disagree with him. My memories of that time are, in the main, happy and wholesome ones as was, probably, the case with many of my contemporaries. Others may choose to differ and maybe with good reasons and it certainly wasn't all 'sweetness and light'. My recollections are bound to be conditioned, for good or ill, by the prevailing circumstances and attitudes of the time. If they appear rose-tinted or naive it is probably because, for those short years, I was too busy growing up to take what was happening in the adult world around me too seriously. I believe the experiences of those formative years have their own validity and authenticity and I have tried to describe them from that perspective before the wear and tear and prejudices of later years might have clouded them

George Lyons (front left) with author among a group of Tuam supporters in Croke Park, 1959.

160

over. I hope that the echoes of an older Tuam, which make up these personal recollections, may be informative of an era and an environment that was typical of many Irish towns and which is now only a memory for my generation. I will leave it to the experts to analyse the broader issues which people had to deal with at that time and to make comparisons with the more complex world that we now inhabit.

Tuam is now a very different place to the town I left in 1952. The only time that I got an opportunity to work there was later in that year when I was transferred back, with six other 'recruits', to work in the Beet Office at the railway station for approximately 2 months under the baton of Paddy Rutledge. For the next decade and a bit I worked for CIE in various capacities in many other places, in a dozen counties, before departing to 'fresh fields and pastures new'. During more than six decades since leaving Tuam there have been many twists and turns along the way and I have met and worked and made friends with many interesting people and been involved with many organisations on that journey but I am glad that I have managed to keep in touch with a place that, for me, has always beckoned, albeit at a distance.

Acknowledgements

I wish to thank the following people for providing access to photographs which I have used in this publication:

Anne Tierney of OTS, Willie Douglas, P.J. Grealish, Donal Igoe, Rosaleen Flanagan, my sister-in-law, Nuala, my sister, Eileen and my niece, June Lavelle. In the same context I remember, with gratitude, two friends who are no longer with us, Ronnie Conlon and Fr Sean Higgins.

I would like to thank Ted Hurley for giving me access to programs of theatrical events in Tuam which helped to fill gaps in my own collection and Mary Trayers for providing me with some early school data.

I wish to thank Tony Varley for reading the text and for his positive comments.

I am very grateful to Riana O'Dwyer for her comprehensive and encouraging feedback which I much appreciate.

As always, the *Tuam Herald* has been an invaluable source of information for which I am extremely grateful. I also found the *Clár Cuimhneacháin* of the Official Opening of Tuam Stadium in 1950 a useful source of information.

I wish to thank Geraldine Kane of Stone Lakes Design for her assistance with the layout and cover design.

I would also like to thank Josephine, Michael and Brendan for their support at all times.